THE GLORY THAT WAS HOME

THE GLORY THAT WAS HOME

BRIAN TOWNSEND

LOCHAR PUBLISHING • MOFFAT • SCOTLAND

© BRIAN TOWNSEND 1990

Published by Lochar Publishing Ltd

Designed by Hammond Hammond

British Library Cataloguing in Publication Data
Townsend, Brian
  The glory that was home.
  1. Great Britain. Stately homes
  I. Title
  941

ISBN 0-948403-31-4

Picture credits
Black and white photographs reproduced with the kind permission of the following:

SAVE, National Heritage, Aberdeen Journals and the Royal Commission on Ancient and Historical Monuments of Scotland.

Colour photographs of Eilean Aigas, Charlton, Kinkeil, Glenmayne, Islay House and Paxton by Eric Thorburn.

CONTENTS

INTRODUCTION

HE BRITISH COUNTRY house, popularly called the stately home, is arguably Britain's greatest contribution to cultural and architectural history. Whereas in almost all other European countries, the wealthy lived and died in the cities, the rich of Britain – and in particular England – had an enduring love and fascination for the countryside. They had fine, but rarely ostentatious, houses in town, and put all their wealth and creativity into their country houses.

The results over many centuries were both remarkable and fascinating. British country houses displayed a variety and vitality of style, architecture, interior decoration and quality of finish which few other countries could match. Those who had money brought in architects, engineers, designers, landscape architects, gardeners and skilled craftsmen from all over Britain and Europe to build houses which outshone those within the shire, and well beyond it, and created a tradition and a uniquely British cultural heritage that still profoundly influences us today.

However, just as Spain grew rich in the sixteenth and seventeenth centuries from assets and gold taken from those civilisations it conquered in Latin America – but fell into decline once those sources of wealth were depleted – so the British country house flourished and waned.

Essentially, the country house was the opulent, rich kernel of a relatively feudal and hierarchical system of land ownership. This provided a large estate peopled by tenant farmers whose rents provided the income to keep the house and all that went with it operating. When, in the course of the last century, that feudal system eventually broke down, so did the country house.

The result was that, from the late nineteenth century onwards, the great country houses started to become non-viable. That non-viability became decline and decline eventually became death. Between 1870 and the present day, more than 2000 in Britain were destroyed, demolished, blown up or bulldozed – or somehow conveniently caught fire and were never rebuilt.

This book looks at the reasons and the background to that decline in some detail, and takes a closer look at several houses whose disappearance gives the greatest cause for dismay. But we also look at ten country houses which have been rescued from final ruin and are being, or have been, lovingly restored thanks to the tenacity and determination of individuals.

Some of the houses we chronicle are being, or have been, brought back to life by companies – but even there it has often been the vision or determination of an individual within the company which

A masterpiece in brass – the great lion door knocker at the east entrance of Plas Teg, North Wales.

The impressive black marble staircase at Hamilton Palace, which was removed before the house was demolished in the 1920s after the foundations had been rendered unsafe by mineworkings in the Lanarkshire coalfield.

A panorama of fine plasterwork at Chatelherault, Lanarkshire. Beautfiful dentilled cornices, intricate ceilings and complex wall-frieze all add to the magnificent effect, lit by the central chandelier. (Above)

has proved the crucial catalyst to the project.

This is not a book aimed at a specialist or devotee audience of connoisseurs of the subject. It is aimed at people who are interested in and enjoy visiting country houses or fine buildings, such as those belonging to the National Trust, and those who occasionally toy with the idea of using their nest egg to buy and restore a listed building but have always thought it beyond them.

The experiences related in this book, of people who have set off down that road, may make that task seem even more daunting, or put one off altogether. On the other hand, the difficulties they encountered provide a bedrock of experience which may ensure that those who follow in their footsteps have an easier journey.

If this book inspires even one person to take up such a challenge and see the restoration task through to a successful completion, then it will have been well worth writing.

PART ONE

LAYING
FOUNDATIONS

VER SINCE PEOPLE moved out of caves and built dwellings, men and women have thought up ways of improving them. Equally, since the development of civilisation, society has become stratified – there have been the mighty and the humble, the wealthy and the poor, the leaders and the led. Somehow those who were at the top of the social tree have wanted to display their prominence by living in better houses than those of ordinary people. To live in a fine dwelling has at one time or another been the leading aspiration of many if not most people on this planet.

The development of the country house in Britain, particularly in England, stems from two separate historical developments. One was the gradual decline of warfare which rendered the need for castles and fortified dwellings superfluous. The other was the establishment and growth of an aristocracy who had land, possibly given to an ancestor by the monarch in reward for loyalty and deeds done, and who increasingly had the opportunity to travel to Europe and marvel at its cities and historic civilisations.

On such visits, many were impressed by the art and sculpture, the layout and design, the contrast of buildings and gardens, and by the sheer historical and cultural magnificence of certain cities, particularly in Italy and Greece.

One of the things we tend to forget now – if indeed we ever gave it a thought – was that until the nineteenth century and the industrial revolution, Britain was regarded by many Continental people as a bit of an offshore backwater and cultural blackspot. Even when England, later Britain, became a powerful seafaring nation and started to establish colonies, it was still regarded on the Continent as culturally inferior.

Although we do not realise it, there are still vestiges of these attitudes prevalent in modern times. Much of General de Gaulle's hostility to Britain's entry into the European Economic Community (EEC) in the 1960s stemmed from this attitude rather than from wholly political considerations. Some,

Rankeillour House, near Lupar, Fife. Square, almost bland mansion, but with an amazing Baroque extension with ornate portico and cupola. Demolished 1956. (Left)

The Jacobean, Georgian and Victorian facades of Stocken Hall, Leicestershire – hemmed in by other development it is unlikely to attract a restorer.

indeed many, of the differences Britain has with her partners in the EEC stem too from this 'culture gap'.

In Britain, there is an almost unconscious tendency to concede that point, and look up to things emanating from Europe as being superior to that which we make at home. On a very simple level, we still tend to 'look up' to wine-drinking and down on beer drinking – because wine-drinking is and was prevalent on the Continent, and wine-drinking for generations was the prerogative of the well-to-do who had travelled abroad. Similar attitudes still prevail towards, say, Cognac and French cuisine: they are viewed as innately superior to our own spirits and home cooking. And as recently as the 1930s, many so-called upper-class families would speak French to each other – so servants and tradespeople would not understand what was being said.

Almost all Britons who travelled to Europe in past centuries, be it to study, or to perform diplomacy and state business, were from the aristocracy and their entourage. They became aware, or were made to feel aware by their hosts, of the cultural gap between the best in Europe and in Britain. Over the decades and centuries, it became *de rigeur* for the scions of aristocratic families to do the 'grand tour' of Europe, learning languages and steeping themselves in the history and culture of their host nation. They saw and marvelled at the buildings and palazzos they visited. And if they had the money, many of them set about building copies and replicas once they returned to Britain.

It was the embodiment of those two old sayings that all good ideas travel and that imitation is the sincerest form of flattery. But what was to happen in Britain was unique.

First, these houses were mostly to be built in rural settings, not spaced out in rows along splendid Roman *vias* or French *boulevards* and *chaussées*. This meant their owners and creators could, and would, attach as much importance to the landscape in which the house was set as to the house itself.

Second, it sparked rivalry among aristocratic

families, with the new splendour of Stromdale Hall prompting Astonbury Saye over the hill to be pulled down and magnificently rebuilt. Bloxton Manor ten miles away, similarly had its perfectly fine Elizabethan facade demolished to be replaced by a Jacobean or Palladian frontage.

Third, was the creation of several generations of outstanding British architects and interior designers, landscape architects and surveyors, who conceived, designed and supervised the construction of many country houses, and a parallel growth in numbers and repute of fine craftsmen and tradesmen who carried out the work. In turn, the skills of some of these people brought them custom from overseas, and a few moved to the New World and worked there or, on rare occasions, were in demand on the continent of Europe.

Social historians will, rightly, point out that families squandered fortunes to build or rebuild country houses on a grand, indeed lavish, scale at a time when the tenants on their estates lived in poverty and squalor in neglected farms and cottages, and that rents and other heavy demands were placed on them to finance the building and upkeep of a country house into which they would hardly ever be allowed to set foot.

In many instances that was true, but for the most part the British aristocracy and landed gentry ran their estates well by the norms of the times and looked after their estate tenants. After all, it was in the family's long-term interests to see that the estate was kept up, that farmers could pay their rents and that servants were retained for as long as possible. Indeed, the fact there was never anything like the French Revolution in Britain stemmed largely from the strictly-defined, rigidly class-conscious but generally workable, relationship maintained for generations between estate owners and their tenants.

This relationship was helped by the fact that most families stayed in their country houses and saw what was happening on the estates. The problem in other countries, particularly in France, came largely from an aristocracy who lived constantly in town, neglected their

estates but still sought to squeeze as much revenue out of them as possible, often entrusting them to be run by people who exploited their positions of power.

One should not sentimentalise too much on the positive aspects of the way British estates were run, but the fact is they worked and they allowed a benignly feudal system to endure far beyond its time. Indeed, there are still countless estates in operation today which should long since have disappeared – and their survival is a tribute to the enduring quality of a quaint system which only the British could have made to work for so long.

However, two things were to happen in the nineteeth century which were to spell the end of many estates and which led to the long dark night of destruction for many country houses. One was the industrial revolution, which changed Britain from an almost wholly rural society into a near-totally urban one. The other was the agricultural blight of the 1870s. Country houses as the hubs of great estates usually survived one or other of these events. Few survived both unscathed.

Bettisfield Park, near Hanmer lies in a little pocket of Wales enclosed on three sides by Shropshire and is one of Cornelia Bayley's restoration projects.

Nostell Priory, a masterpiece by James Paine who was one of several generations of outstanding British architects which grew up in response to the demand for stately homes. (Left)

WANING FORTUNES

 LTHOUGH MOST OF us rarely give the cost involved in the upkeep of our modest homes too much thought, it would be quite an eye-opener if we actually kept detailed accounts over a year, or a decade, meticulously noting everything we spent on them; repainting the external woodwork every few years; decorating each room on a rota basis; installing central heating or double glazing; laying tarmac in the driveway; putting electrics and a tap in the garage. Then add the electricity, gas, water and sewerage bills, plus a percentage of our rates which cover rubbish removal and maintaining the street on to which the house faces.

If you added it all up, you would be staggered at the final bill. It could well run into thousands of pounds per annum. Now, multiply that bill n-fold and you start to understand the upkeep costs of a great country house.

There were many factors which multiplied the costs of running and maintaining such a home. Let us look at just one aspect: heating. There was the cost of the tons of coal and logs needed to keep fires going for much of the year in dozens of fireplaces. The logs may well have been 'free', coming from woodlands on the estate – but it took time and much effort to cut, saw, move, dry and store them.

Then there would be the staff and time needed to take the coal and logs to every room in the house, to set every fire and laboriously clean it out each day, to ensure the ashes were scattered or buried. As if all this were not enough, the chimney sweep had to be brought in, possibly with an apprentice, twice a year to clean the dozens of flues. Inevitably this created more cleaning after he had gone.

This complicated, labour-intensive system of running the house applied to every other aspect – washing, cleaning, cooking, food-preserving, external and internal maintenance. Even lighting, which meant maintaining dozens of oil lamps or candles and candlesticks, could keep one member of the domestic staff occupied up for several hours a day.

Staff wages were poor, indeed abysmal – but staff got their food, keep, laundry and other odds and ends, which in a big household could add far more to costs than merely counting the costs of staff wages. In short, running a country house was like running a big hotel – but with no paying guests

House of Gray, near Dundee. Built 1715 by the 10th Lord Gray, the house lay a gutted ruin for several decades, but it is now being restored by an Edinburgh company. Pictured in 1965.

coming to call. To keep the house going called for a large and continuous income.

That income came largely, if not entirely, from the estate in the shape of rent from the tenant farmers. Indeed the whole concept of the country house was based on there being large amounts of land from which to derive that income. Historians on either side of the political median line will argue at great length about the benevolence or tyranny of this system, but the fact was that for many centuries it worked.

The reason lay less in the rewards of being a tenant farmer than in the fact there were few alternatives. Nowadays we take it totally for granted that if we do not like working for one employer, we can move to another; if we do not like a town, we can move elsewhere. But in those days, things for the humbler strata of society were very different. In a nutshell, there was nowhere else to go. The occasional prodigal son could uproot and set off, Dick Whittington-like, to seek his fortune in London or the New World, but for many people life was stuck in the rural rut.

Things changed, and radically, with the industrial revolution. It wasn't called that then, but word reached even the most isolated of rural communities that there were jobs and prospects in the burgeoning cities and

Guys Cliffe House, Warwick pictured in a delapidated state of final collapse – despite its status as a Grade 1 listed building.

factories. In the wake of the magic steam engine, which – it was said – could do all the hard labour and transform the lives of everyone, thousands moved to the mill towns and growing centres of industrial activity.

Many of those who uprooted from the countryside and moved into town had long and deep reason to regret their move, as they encountered squalor and financial deprivation worse than that left behind them. But for every man who gave up and returned to his rural roots, there were scores more, who stayed in the towns and new industries. They in turn fetched their womenfolk from their home villages and hamlets to join them.

The same phenomenon happens today, only on a global scale. Young men from Third-World countries move to the developed world or to the oil-rich countries of the Middle East, find work, settle down and bring their wives, girlfriends or fiancees to join them – local circumstances and legislation permitting of course.

From the 1820s on, there was a gradual loss of manpower from the great estates, as young men moved to the cities. Estate cottages and farms slowly but inexorably emptied. Estate owners fell back on two remedies, cutting back where they could and pushing up rents to make up the shortfall caused by the departing or deceased tenants. That only increased the pressure on those tenants who remained – and who in turn would look with increasing attention to the temptations and prospects of industry and the cities.

With the benefit of hindsight, we can ask why the owners of stately homes and estates did not take appropriate steps to save the situation rather than, in many instances, to aggravate it. One answer lies simply in human nature. It is easier to overspend than save – and when spending exceeds income, it is instinctive to seek ways to augment income than to cut expenditure.

A modern parallel is the problem which affected, and sometimes still affects, local authorities who faced a steep decline in their local industries. Many such authorities continued to spend at or above previous levels and increased rates sharply to finance that expenditure.

This would hit the remaining local industries, many of which were increasingly outdated or non-viable, forcing many of them to close down. As factories and warehouses shut their doors, so the rate-base of the local authority shrank, prompting another rise in rates and another round of closures.

To some extent, local authorities were tied to much of that expenditure by legislation or commitment, but too many authorities saw industrial and commercial ratepayers as a cow which could be forever milked, rather than recognising that many were businesses on the margin to whom one more rate rise spelled the end of their commercial viability.

Something of this nature befell estates in the mid-nineteenth century, but many struggled on and survived. Agriculture became more efficient, thanks to the discoveries of 'Turnip' Townshend and others. He found that he could improve his land by good rotation of crops, and earned his nickname by growing large quantities of turnips. Better agricultural practice increased food output and reduced manpower needs.

Certain country house-owning families married their sons and daughters to progeny of the *nouveaux-riches* from industry and commerce. Others married among themselves less for love and family similarity than for sheer economic survival – a wealthy family would hopefully have the resources to keep two estates going instead of one. Some families finished up with more country houses than they knew what to do with.

However, things were going downhill. Quite apart from the loss of manpower to work the farms, young womenfolk were departing for the cities as well. The days when the only option before marriage for a non- or poorly-educated girl was going into service at the hall or the manor were ending. Girls could join their menfolk in town, and sometimes obtain work in the factories or domestic employment among the growing urban middle classes.

But throughout the mid-nineteenth century things kept ticking – until the great farming blight of the 1860s

Another of the fireplaces at Chatelherault, Hamilton Palace – in convex marble with blue-veined white marble enhanced by blue and white tiling. (Left)

A fireplace in the now-restored former hunting lodge of Hamilton Palace, Lanarkshire. The fireplace is surmounted by Adam-style plasterwork and a 'built-in' picture.

and 1870s. There were many causes for the situation which arose. Among the most significant was that the agricultural industry of the New World, combined with new ways of preserving food and transporting it across the Atlantic in steam-driven cargo ships, meant imported food and raw materials were cheaper than home-grown. Farmers could not sell their produce, their income plummeted and many were unable to continue. They uprooted, either to the cities or to the New World, leaving empty farmhouses and unpaid rents. As a result many of the great estates and country houses started to be neglected.

THE LONG JOURNEY INTO NIGHT

NE SHOULD NOT conclude that all estates and country houses were equally hit, or that all the aristocracy and landed gentry stood paralysed by these new circumstances.

Many saw what was coming and took steps to preserve what they had. One such measure – already long in existence – was primogeniture, which ensured the estate always passed on death of the family head to the eldest son. Other sons, although they would doubtless receive good educations and financial support in their early years, had to go out and fend for themselves. Daughters could not inherit estates, nor could illegitimate children – a state of affairs which led to many an aristocratic household being peopled by a platoon of daughters until at last, with both parents exhausted and ailing, a son was born.

The aim of primogeniture was simply to keep the estates intact. In many other countries, it was quite normal for estates to be divided up among all the children after their parents' deaths – but not in Britain.

Many younger sons lived and died in relative poverty or penury, though many fared very well in the armed forces, government service, the Church or whatever. But there was a distinct dearth of them in industry and commerce, as it was considered not to be an acceptable profession for a gentleman.

In a way, that was a pity – because had some of them gone into industry and commerce, they might have learned ideas of management and financial control which, even by the simple norms of those times, would have helped them to avoid or avert the fate that was stalking the family estate.

Even though it was an estate they were not due to inherit – they could have passed many useful thoughts on to their elder brother. Also, not infrequently, the eldest son predeceased his father, or died without children, so the estate did pass to one of the younger sons.

Apart from primogeniture, esates had other defences. They could sell off paintings, jewellery and

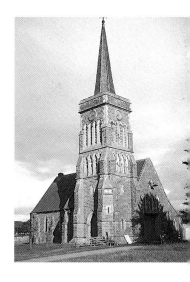

Baron Hall, Anglesey, less lucky than Trevor Hall, it has not found a devoted restorer and is one of many Georgian houses in Wales falling into ruin. (Left)

Duncrub Chapel, Dunning, Perthshire: All that remains of Duncrub, a huge many-spired Gothic mansion in bull-faced masonry. Demolished in 1950.

other valuables, however reluctantly. They could sell the family silver. They could sell individual farms on the estate to the sitting tenant who, by diligence, foresight or sheer acumen, had saved enough to buy it. Or they could sell a farm to an outside purchaser. But both were steps the estate often rued. It fragmented the estate and, although it provided capital at a time of need, it terminated a source of income which might be needed even more in the future.

Splitting up the estate had another adverse effect. Depending on where the sold farms or smallholdings lay, they could disrupt the entity of the estate. Whereas the big map in the factor's office had been an organic whole with everything within the red boundary line part of the estate, that map became a patchwork quilt of bits that belonged and bits that didn't, with rights of way, shared roads and paths and other complications.

These made the total estate a much less attractive proposition when the dark day came and the whole estate had to be put up for sale. Just as a house with bits missing from it, or a row of cottages with several sitting tenants, is a less attractive purchase than a complete freehold, so an estate with parts sold fetched a disproportionately lower price than one still intact.

An additional fact was that the lure of the cities had also infected the young aristocracy. The family pile in the country was perhaps magnificent but it was miles from anywhere and the real social scene was in London which could now be reached quickly and conveniently by train. The drift from the land had reached its pinnacle. Many country houses were becoming unoccupied.

Estates were being sold to company directors and textile magnates, bankers and armaments manufacturers, railway tycoons and beer barons. They, after all, had the income to keep up such large places and were not dependent on farm rentals as income. The rents were a welcome extra, but certainly not essential to the estate's survival.

There were not enough magnates and tycoons available to soak up all the estates which were by then in

difficulty. Some estates were advertised for rent to groups of businessmen, or anyone, for shooting or hunting parties or for country holidays and retreats. Several country houses were used for a few weeks of the year in this way, but it still meant that for most of the year the buildings were unoccupied. As a result some owners looked at the books and came to the regretful conclusion that there was no future in keeping the house going and decided to pull it down.

The Montrose mansion, House of Dun is unusual in that the house has an immediately adjacent courtyard with a central raised game larder and all estate offices and stores next to the house itself.

House of Dun, a recently-restored Adam mansion near Montrose – a fortunate survivor which has weathered the decline in its fortunes. (Left)

TERMINAL DECLINE

THE MAN WHO has the unenviable privilege of being the first country house owner known to opt for demolition was Henry Vyner, and it is significant that he was a relative newcomer, not the latest descendant in a long aristocratic dynasty. He demolished Newby Hall in Lincolnshire in 1872, not realising the long chain-reaction he was setting up.

From that day on, the demolition of the country house appeared to be the only way out. From being the centre of a unique and prestigious world, the country house became an anachronism, a white elephant, an edifice and a concept which had no relevance to the world. There were other factors, too, which were to change things further, such as the introduction of income tax and death duties – two measures which were aimed at the wealthy, or by now the once-wealthy, as they were intended to.

Death duties were to fall severely, if unintentionally, on certain families during the First World War. Although it was not the intention of the legislators – who primarily wished to see primogeniture diminished so that the assets of a family were spread more evenly among the descendants – the results were far more drastic than expected following the huge loss of life, even among the upper classes, in that war. Huge death duties fell on those families who lost a son, or several sons, during the war, obliging the families to sell entire estates. If there were no buyers for the country house, it was pulled down to save on staffing, rates and upkeep.

This long saga of destruction has lasted almost to the present day – and is a cause for national dismay. More than 2000 country houses have been demolished since 1870, with particular bursts of destruction following both world wars and during the 1960s. It was only the now-famous exhibition held at the Victoria and Albert Museum in 1974, and the book *The Destruction of the Country House* published the following year, that finally aroused public attention and showed how the country house had become an endangered species.

A decade or two later we can say that, at long last, the country house demolition derby appears to be at its end, but it was a close-run thing. Looking back over the earlier years of this century, it must have seemed that Britain was determined to eradicate the country house from this island.

It is an interesting point that, although we accept that country houses were marvels of architecture

A victim of the long chain-reaction set up by Henry Vyne, Caldecote House, Herts, which once boasted a fascinating facade with artificial quoins used to emphasise the serliana window above the porch, has been demolished. (Left)

Abercairny House, Near Crieff. Another great Gothick mansion built in finely-wooded grounds in 1842 and enlarged in 1873. Demolished in 1960.

*L*indertis, near Kirriemuir, Tayside: Rebuilt 1813 as a Gothick castellated mansion, finally gutted in 1955. The contrast betweeen the house in its heyday, 1920, and the empty shell, 1956, speaks for itself.

and interior decoration and often stood in the midst of landscaped gardens and woodlands of breathtaking beauty, we haven't quite accepted that they only *really* worked when they were residences for families deeply rooted in the place and who devoted much time and effort to running them. Once they were gone, all too many country houses became great piles of masonry with no viable purpose.

Nonsense, would be an instant reply. There are a hundred good uses for them – as boarding schools and other training institutions, as hospitals, hotels, nursing homes, homes for the elderly, training centres, offices and so on and so forth.

However, experience has shown that this is not always the case. Indeed, certain country houses have

*S*tracathro House is an
outstanding Palladian
mansion with a magnificent
portico and a pediment with
two lovely side pavilions.

A fine house adversely
affected by institutional
use – Stracathro House, Angus.
Used since the war as a
hospital, it stands at the end of
an avenue of prefabricated low-
rise hospital buildings.

been ruined far more rapidly by institutional use than had they simply stood empty. The examples are both numerous and edifying.

First, almost no institutional user has been able to utilise the country house it acquired as it stood. Sweeping changes needed to be made to internal layouts to render the place usable. Great rooms were split up to form smaller offices or classrooms, and were split up on the cheap. Simple plasterboard or boxboard partitions were placed across rooms, breaking up the fine plasterwork or cornices. Beautiful fireplaces were blanked off. Stairways and corridors, designed with perspective and intended to enchant the eye, were chopped and changed to accommodate fire doors and other requirements.

Bedrooms, which were too big to be viable in a hotel where bed-nights and floor space must earn money had to be split and bathrooms installed. These required extensive plumbing, which could not all be concealed behind existing walls. And a hundred and one other changes had to be made, most or all of which adversely affected the interior decoration and layout.

Second, institutional use meant great changes externally. Fire escapes often had to be installed – and an attractive fire escape is one invention no architect or engineer has yet devised. In the twenteith century, any building which attracted a large number of people on a daily basis needed parking facilities. Human laziness being what it is, those car-parks needed to be close by, often ensuring that what had been a lovely edifice in a swirling green sea of trimmed lawn became just another

*D*unglas House, East Lothian – windows deprived of glass expose the interior to all elements.

building ringed by tarmac at night and a motley mosaic of parked cars during the day.

Institutional use brought one further problem. Institutions – whether public or private – tended to grow and, however large the country house they moved into, they needed more space. Land here was no problem, but extensions were. The institutions, in applying for planning permission to extend, usually submitted plans for simple modern extensions, as building modern replica extensions of the original edifice were too expensive.

Until quite recently, almost all planning authorities would grant such extensions, though some would insist their being built as separate annexes so the constructional entity of the country house was untouched. This was fine, but it meant the house gradually became lost in a growing township of other, modern buildings which bore no resemblance or organic similarity to the country house they besieged.

This happened particularly during and after the Second World War – and it was usually done, or caused, by the armed forces or government departments. The problem is not so much the period during which the institution is alive and flourishing. It is what happens when the hospital or school either closes down or moves to more modern or more central premises elsewhere – abandoning the country house in its sea of prefabs and jerry-built extensions.

Tragically, these are among the country houses most

at risk. Virtually nobody wants them. They are totally without interest to the private purchaser, who would have to spend a fortune bulldozing the extensions and re-landscaping the area around the main house, in addition to the fortune that would have to be spent on the house itself to 'rescue' it from all the institutional 'improvements' inflicted on it over the years. Developers might be interested, but would want to demolish the house along with the prefabs to ensure a 'clean site' for the housing scheme they have in mind.

Having said this, it must be stressed that many country houses have been saved by being put to institutional use, and many more have been saved by companies and organisations buying them to use as their head offices or as training schools for executive or technical staff. Other companies have bought them as special retreats where phone-harrassed executives and senior management can spend an uninterrupted weekend planning corporate strategy.

But such company-acquired country houses tend to be among the smaller ones and lie close to the Home Counties or other main centres of population, or at least close to airports and motorways. Country houses far from the madding crowd tend not to be in demand for these purposes.

It should also be said that as the twentieth century has progressed, building, fire, safety and other legislation has made the purchase and conversion of country houses to institutional use increasingly non-viable. Hotel chains, which are as cost-conscious and businesslike as any commercial organisation, have found that the cost of installing modern plumbing facilities, fire doors and escapes into an existing building, even one bought cheaply, far outweighs the costs of building from scratch.

The same applies to nursing homes and residential homes for the elderly: fire legislation here is even more stringent, and only low-rise new buildings are really viable except in dense urban areas where there are fewer country houses anyway.

That fact raises another point. Except where country houses have gradually been surrounded by suburbs as the result of urban growth, many tend to be in relatively isolated locations. This reduces their attraction to, for instance, nursing home or old folks' home operators. It may well be difficult to attract staff, or costly to provide transport. Also, the relatives of residents may not be too eager to place them in homes which are too remote and thus prevent easy visiting, even by car.

If anything, therefore, institutional use of former country houses is on the wane. What has supplanted it is the concept of converting them into several residences, ranging from simple one or two-bedroomed flats to vast five-bedroomed, three-bathroomed homes, with maximum privacy and as little alteration to the house structure, especially externally, as possible. Such conversions will be looked at in later chapters.

North Barningham Hall, Norfolk is the sort of house for which there is now a logical market. It would not be too difficult to restore, is not too large and is within possible commuting distance of London.

A PARADIGM
OF LOSS

T WOULD BE incorrect to assume that converting old country houses to smaller units is a new idea. There are many examples of such conversions being done over the past century. Originally, these tended to be the hiving off and sale of a wing or section of a country house by a family whose fortunes had shrunk so far they were down just to the house and a few surrounding acres.

However, since the Second World War, some houses have been converted into flats. In some isolated instances, these post-war conversions were well conceived, the workmanship good and the end result quite effective. But more often than not, the conversion was poorly thought out, the work bad and the end result diabolical. A classic example was Hammerwood Park, which has now thankfully been restored to an entity by its current owner.

One reason for much poor conversion work was that the owners were often so often short of money they tried to do things on the cheap. Also, they rarely had a plan for maintaining the building once the conversion was done. The flats were rented out, but little thought was given to maintaining the grounds, or even the external structure of the house, beyond the bare minimum.

All too often, therefore, the country house continued to decay, even though it was occupied. Once a house starts to fall into decay and dereliction, it becomes an accelerating process. Good tenants move out and sometimes less careful ones move in. They tend to push out the remaining better tenants, and so the cycle of decline continues.

Other factors in the cycle of decline were local authorities. Many were for years totally unsympathetic to owners of problem houses, insisting on repairs and maintenance while still keeping rents controlled at totally unremunerative levels. Yet owners driven to apply for permission to demolish usually had their applications refused.

Legislation aimed at protecting Britain's heritage often only complicated matters. Although much of the legislation was passed with the best of intentions, it put many fine country houses into a hopeless limbo, a legal swampland where the owner could not move in any direction without being in danger of immediately sinking.

There are as many examples of the problem as there are country houses. But let's just take

Fetteresso Castle, near Stonehaven in Grampian. A large, rambling, gutted shell which fell into disrepair after World War II and was deroofed in the 1960s to avoid rates. (Left)

Douglas Castle, Lanarkshire. A seat of the Douglas-Holmes, the castle was only one-eighth of its originally planned size. The building originally had flat-topped castellated towers, but the pointed, almost minaret-style towers were added about the turn of this century. Demolished 1939 – the M74 motorway now cuts through the estate.

a fictitious example called Doomladen Hall. A great Georgian pile with a magnificent Palladian pediment, forty or more huge rooms, numerous outhouses and acres of surrounding parkland, it gradually became unoccupied during the 1920s and 1930s as the family fortunes declined. It was located in remote fenland, too far from London to find a buyer, especially as most of the estate was sold off and fields were being ploughed within forty yards of the front door.

The house was requisitioned by the RAF during the Second World War and, although it was quite well maintained, a great deal of hurried, ill-thought out alterations were done and a host of Nissen huts and prefabs built all around. The RAF left in 1950 and,

Although currently a soot-blackened and abandoned shell Clegg Hall, Rochdale may be saved by the Pennine Trust.

luckily, the premises were taken over as a boys' preparatory school. More alterations and modifications were made to adapt Doomladen Hall to its new role, and things ran well for fifteen years.

Then the school hit bad times, a damaging story appeared in the Sunday papers and parents pulled their children out and sent them elsewhere. The house stood empty for two years, then was taken over by two businessmen who asset-stripped the place, selling fine panelling to US buyers, fireplaces to builders who were restoring some big houses thirty miles away, and some of the original outbuildings to buyers for residential or other use.

The stables were taken over by a motor racing team who had permission to use the nearby disused RAF airfield as a test circuit. They attracted a pile of motor racing and motor trade-related businesses to Doomladen, all of them setting up in the ex-RAF prefabs and elsewhere. The house remained unoccupied, although some of the traders kept car spares and old tyres in some of the downstairs rooms and cellars.

Spares, oil, tyres and timber proved a combustible mix and a forgotten cigarette left smouldering set the whole lot alight. Two fifths of the house burned down in the summer of 1973.

For three years, things went from bad to worse. The boss of the racing team was killed in a car crash, and the team folded. So did most of the little businesses which survived only on the business the racing team brought. As they closed down or moved on, they left huge mounds of automotive detritus and Doomladen looked every inch its name. Although it was three miles from the nearest small town, the neglected place soon attracted vandals who broke in, smashed windows and did untold damage.

The local authority, who had ignored the problem of Doomladen for as long as they could, were finally prodded into action after four young children, who had entered the derelict place out of curiosity, fell twelve feet through a rotting floor into the hall below. One died.

The place was boarded up and the council set out to

enforce a repairs notice on the owners. That task almost defeated the skills of the council's legal department, who discovered that ownership of the property was almost impossible to resolve, bits and pieces having been sold off to other people and even the main building nominally owned by a defunct partnership of the two businessmen, one of whom had emigrated and the other landed in jail. But they managed to piece the mosaic together. Not that it helped the repairs notice – the jailed businessman had no assets to pay for the repairs.

A spark of hope glimmered in 1982 or 1983 when a consortium said they would buy the property and convert it into a restaurant, hotel and golf course to cater for the growing leisure market in the area. The offer, which was hailed in the local Press as the breakthrough that would finally restore Doomladen to its former and long-forgotten glory, was subject to two conditions – that land to form the golf course would be made available and that planning and other necessary permissions be granted.

That was where it all came unstuck. The land purchase for the golf course proved relatively easy, but everything else did not. The district authority, delighted to get this festering sore off their books, were also keen enough to grant planning permission. But goodwill and good intentions were not enough. The county council, as roads authority, rejected the new access road and its feedout on to the main trunk road and also rejected an alternative roads proposal from the consortium. Asked to provide a – to them – acceptable alternative, the county council suggested a road line which cut the golf course into two and was rejected by the consortium as defeating the purpose of the exercise.

The fire authority stipulated stringent fire safety requirements for the building, including metal external stairs and many internal fire doors. The Georgian Society, who for years had lamented Doomladen's decline, objected strongly to the damage they claimed the fire requirements would do to the building's appearance and opposed the consortium's plan to build a twenty-

four-bedroom extension at the side which, they pointed out, would be totally out of keeping with the Palladian symmetry of the frontage.

Just to complicate matters further, one of the long-lost owners of the outbuildings, who had lain low while the repairs notice was being served but popped up when there was money to be made, demanded an absolutely ridiculous price for his little patch. Two cottage owners, who would be affected by the conversion of Doomladen to its new role, objected to aspects of the project.

None of the hurdles, however irritating, were insurmountable. But they proved immensely costly and time-consuming to the consortium, who persevered for nearly a year – but gave up when one of the big hotel chains won approval for a rival project on a greenfield site eight miles away. The plan collapsed.

Since then the local authority have been hunting for someone to take over Doomladen. All these years later, it is still boarded up, increasingly vandalised – though less

*U*pper Shibden Hall, Halifax although an unlisted ruin it would be a worthwhile restoration project. It has a Sir John Soane style bow front and a campanile-style tower.

so since the roof in the section untouched by the fire collapsed from years of dry rot. A few individuals and organisations have shown interest now and again, but are put off by the increasingly astronomical cost of restoring the building and memories of the problems which defeated the consortium. The house may well rot indefinitely.

For every Doomladen Hall, there are a dozen real-life examples one could quote, whose stories are every bit as desperate and absurd. But there are local authorities, conservation bodies, private individuals and organisations who work hard to rescue country houses in peril – and to reconcile the conflicting requirements of legislation and conservation, expediency and authenticity and above all budgets and timetables.

Often the success stories pass unnoticed and forgotten, while the failures stick up from the landscape like giant tombstones.

Eilean Aigas: Located on an island in the River Beauly, Inverness-shire, this retreat of Lord Lovat was once the summer residence of Sir Robert Peel. Great houses were designed with the concept of one room passing into another, as the interior of Eilean Aigas carefully illustrates.

*F*alling further and further into disrepair, Yeaton Peavery is a relatively recent nineteenth century, Jacobean-style manor. It is however, still in a redeemable condition.

*T*he main south facade of Castle Howard (far left) – with its great nine-bay central block surmounted by turrets and the great central cupola. Above, the western block of the Castle Howard stables, doubtless used as offices or stores. Left, the west facade of Castle Howard, showing (from bottom to top) a double door with fanlight surmounted by a semi-circle of keystones forming a perfect arch.

*H*igh Head was destroyed by fire in 1956, and has remained an abandoned shell since – it is at last being restored. (Above)

*P*ell Wall Hall, Shropshire. One of the last houses built by the great Sir John Soane, a full restoration is estimated at a cost of £2.5 million. (Right)

*T*he south face of Newburgh Priory, Yorkshire. Displaying a bewildering variety of styles in single frontage. On the far right are the roofless ruins of an early gothic abbey . . . (Far right)

DECAY
AND NEGLECT

NE OF THE things one can so easily forget when looking at a splendid building is that it is essentially a large box made from various materials – primarily timber and either brick or stone – which through human design, ingenuity and craftsmanship, is made into something that pleases the eye and provides a comfortable place in which to live.

Although timber, brick and stone have been the most widely-used building materials over the centuries because of their utility and durability, all of them are far from invulnerable. Many types of stone can weather, crumble and be eaten by atmospheric pollution. Early bricks (which were often poorly fired) would disintegrate if broken and left on exposed faces – and untreated timber, even of best native hardwoods, could deteriorate drastically in certain circumstances. This type of decay happened all too frequently as country houses entered their nemesis years earlier this century.

All buildings, as has been said many times, require constant upkeep. The bigger and more complex the building, the more upkeep and expenditure it requires. It is also a cardinal rule, with country houses, as with other buildings, that prevention is better than cure. But as this century saw their fortunes decline, many families no longer had enough money available even to pay for routine checks, maintenance and repairs.

An architect, one of an enthusiastic partnership which restores stately homes as a commercial operation, explained how decay and downfall could creep unnoticed into a country house structure:

When the country house was occupied and in full swing,' the butler or major-domo could send a house lad up on to the roof twice a year to check slates, lead flashings and chimney pots and to clear the gutters. If he reported anything amiss, a tradesman would be sent up promptly to rectify it. But, as the family fortunes declined, staff left and only the old butler remained. He was unable to go up on the roof. So the gutters got choked and rainwater would seep between the slates and the wallhead and run down the inner face of the outer walls. This seepage might stay unnoticed for years – but the water set up wet rot or, worse, dry rot in the timberwork.

Dry rot is the nastiest of infections – the AIDS or cancer of a fine house. It's a prolific fungus which spreads through every sort of timber, the bigger the better, and which does best in cold, damp, unoccupied and

Charlton, Fife, an unusual design combining the granite-like austerity of Scots manorial design with three or four intriguing details – the portico, the deep alcove with statue above it and the many-hipped dormer window above that. Then there is the modern-looking bow-fronted addition to the right . . .

Almost Adamesque interior, with deep green colouring, mirrors and ormolu plasterwork.

Seggieden, Kinfauns, near Perth: An austere mansion with a fine Hellinic-style extension. Seen four years before its demolition in 1970, it still showed much of its earlier splendour, especially in the Oval Room.

undisturbed areas of a house. It hates warmth and light and, despite its name, needs lots of moisture. It will eat its way through solid stone to reach water. That is why it did such devastating damage to so many stately homes this century – as the family, or what was left of them, retracted more and more into one wing or corner of the house.

Rooms, corridors, entire sections were closed off. Cursory external and internal checks might be made, but all too often they were not. Unknown to the family, roof slates might have been blown away, lead might have rotted through or been stolen by thieves, and water was slowly but relentlessly seeping into structural woodwork, bringing in the dry rot spores or irrigating the dry rot already hard at work.

This would go on for years until, quite suddenly, a weakened main beam would break and an entire ceiling, roof or floor would collapse, demolishing what was beneath it. If – as was usually the case – the main beams and joists acted as bracing for the entire structure, the outer walls cracked, bulged and collapsed either then or shortly afterwards. Houses literally fell down where they stood.

It was a relatively rare occurence that part of a house collapsed with the family in residence – but it is not unknown. If a house had dry rot and other damaging infestations, these would proliferate all the more if the house eventually became unoccupied.

Such houses, as even the most casual observer can testify, deteriorate at a frightening speed. Even remote and isolated ones are vandalised – and ones close to major centres of population suffer severe vandalism even if they are boarded up and otherwise protected. Thieves clamber on to roofs and steal lead flashing, or break in and steal plumbing, fireplaces and any removable interior decor for which there is a market.

Sometimes, the removal of such items was done quite legitimately. Houses were bought by businessmen or developers specifically to asset-strip, in the hope – or sometimes the knowledge – that once the house was sufficiently ruined and vandalised, they could obtain consent for demolition, which would free the land it stood on for other development.

Even where a country house did not fall prey to vandalism or asset-stripping, it could still deteriorate badly without anyone being aware of it. The decay would only come to light when the house, perhaps after years of partial or total abandonment, would be put up for sale. The prospective purchasers would have the house surveyed, discover such horrors that they would decide not to buy. Some bought without an adequate survey and subsequently found dry rot so bad it was beyond their slender means to rectify.

Still others bought country houses with a general awareness of the dry rot and other damage but discovered more and more of it as their renovation work progressed. If they had borrowed from the banks or building societies, or had obtained a grant from English Heritage or its Welsh or Scots counterparts, they all too frequently had to return to those bodies and ask for more money. However, even these agencies do not have bottomless pits of funding.

The second section of this book deals with several houses which fell into decay and eventual collapse. Each example should, hopefully, provide insight into both the circumstances which led to its downfall and the misplaced good intentions to rescue it. Each loss was a tragic story in its own right, often as gripping as the plays, whodunnits and Gothic novels set, by generations of writers, in those same country houses.

A misfield House, Haddington, East Lothian. Built by the fifth Earl of Wemyss between 1787 and 1808 in red sandstone. Demolished 1928.. (Above)

BRICKS
AND MORTAR

LTHOUGH WE WOULD be hard put to realise it, there is a strong and continuous link which connects the early caves of *homo sapiens* with our modern, centrally-heated homes complete with all our modern conveniences. They both provide a place to live.

Even caves possessed certain features which still apply to the most up-to-date dwelling. They offered shelter, protection from the elements and a secure place in which the young could be born and reared. Our ancestors also subdivided the available space into a living area near the cave mouth with a fire to provide heat and light, to cook and to ward off predatory animals, and a sleeping area further in, made more comfortable with dried moss or animal skins.

Where possible, the cave would be close to a water source – either a spring or a river – and sources of food. Although early humans were certainly not houseproud, it is more than likely that steps were taken to remove decaying food remains – such as bones and offal – before their smell and maggots made the cave uninhabitable.

Similarly, there would be an agreed area outside but close to the cave where adults would go to urinate and defecate. It is also known that even the most primitive human beings buried their dead. As people became a bit more advanced, they would draw or paint simple pictures on the cave walls.

What is fascinating about all that is not how primitive it was – but how, in its own simple way, it parallels home life as we know it today.

We still divide our homes into living and sleeping areas, and we still have a main heat source – be it a fire or a central heating boiler – though we tend to have an additional or secondary heat source for cooking. We still take steps to remove food residues, often before they have a chance to go off. We now have a toilet inside the house. But that is a relative newcomer. Until well into this century, toilets for most people tended to be outside affairs, whether in the garden or on the landing of a tenement block – even in Britain.

Admittedly, we do not normally paint pictures on our inner walls, but we put on attractive wallpaper and enhance it with pictures by people more skilled at painting than we are.

However, we need to understand that people's most basic living needs have changed little over the

Pitcorthie House, Fife. Forgotten late-Palladian house with symmetrical wings near Colinsburgh. Demolished 1950. (Left)

Kirklinton House, north-east of Carlisle. Originally a fortified Scots-style Jacobean farmhouse, to which huge extensions were added in the nineteenth century. The huge task of restoration is now underway.

An interesting example of timber-frame building, subsequently harled, with a great fireplace and chimney built on to one wall is provided by Longford Hall, Stretford.

Scout Hall, West Yorkshire is a fascinating house, evidently built to celebrate the scrapping of 'window tax'. Also showing a highly unusual asymmetry.

millennia, only the means and methods of satisfying them have become infinitely more sophisticated. Those means and methods are enshrined in our dwellings – and the creation of, and changes to, our dwellings are a usable yardstick of human civilisation.

In that respect, our development has been patchy and erratic. Leaving aside electricity and gas, most other advanced or sophisticated features of human dwellings have been in existence for thousands of years. The Romans had very effective central heating systems 2000 years before the metal hot-water radiator appeared. On Crete, the Minoans had outstanding water-supply and drainage systems by about 3000BC – though this was in the palace at Knossus: whether the dwellings of ordinary citizens were so equipped we do not know.

Yet the chimney – as distinct from a smoke vent in the roof – did not arrive until the fourteenth century and the development of the modern lavatory dates back not much more than a hundred years. (There were said to be only three or four primitive latrines in the whole of the Palais de Versailles. Providing for human excretory needs always rated a low priority with early architects.)

Equally, the main components of a house – walls, roof, chimneys, windows and doors – have developed and improved only as the materials to build them developed and improved. Some nations and societies identified certain advances and put them to full use earlier than others. We must remember, too, that the difference in living standards between rich and poor, was much wider in the past – so norms for houses built for the upper levels of society might, and did, take centuries to come within the grasp of those less fortunate.

The rich might well have lived superlative lives in magnificent houses with a standard of living as good as, if technically simpler than, that of their descendants today – while poorer people lived nearby in huts of unmortared stones with turf roofs little changed from the dawn of civilisation.

To take one simple example – crude glass was available in Britain from the thirteenth century onwards.

Yet it was not until Elizabethan times, that merchant and middle-class homes had glazed windows and it was another two centuries at least until poorer homes had it installed. Windows in poorer homes were all too often empty gaps clumsily shuttered at night, or were crude wooden frames with a cow's dried placenta stretched across them.

Windows are just one fascinating example of how house design and appearance changed over the centuries to keep pace with what one might call technical improvements. Equally, one has to admire how early architects and craftsmen hatched styles, designs and entire building systems to camouflage the limitations and shortcomings of the materials which with they had to work.

Tudor and earlier housebuilders, for instance, relied largely on timber, usually solid oak, for the main structure and walls of unfortified houses, filling in the gaps between the vertical timbers with mud or clay which was then plastered or painted white both inside and out. Often they found they had large amounts of smaller pieces of timber, perfectly good but insufficient for main structural work. Hence they evolved the system of filling in the gaps between the main vertical timbers with a wooden latticework of symmetrical and decorative patterns – now regarded as the hallmark of the era.

The same applied to their windows. Glassmaking was very primitive and it was impossible to make large sheets. So, again making a virtue out of necessity, complex and often beautiful windows were created by combining dozens of small panes in a lead frame or lattice. It was slow and labour-intensive, but labour was cheap whereas glass and lead were not.

However, the leaded windows would never have stood the strain of being opened and shut like doors. So, once they were fixed in position, that was it. It was only with the much later arrival of wooden-framed sash-weight windows (which moved up and down in their frames, counterbalanced by concealed metal weights) and the modern casement window (which opens on hinges like a door) that opening windows became the norm.

Doors are also an interesting item which developed over the centuries. The earliest doors were large, flat upright stones which could be swivelled and wedged against the door aperture in an attempt to keep out the elements and also as a rudimentary protection against attack. Later, simple wooden doors were developed which were four or five wide vertical planks nailed rigidly to two widely-spaced horizontal ones – a type of door one still finds in older cottages today.

These were fitted with crude, robust wrought-iron hinges – which often stretched across the entire width of the door – and the whole thing was hung from two or three L-shaped hinge pins embedded in the masonry or timber at the side of the door aperture.

Later still, by the seventeenth century, panelled doors were developed and, more significantly, the concept of door frames with doors moving on flat hinges affixed to the frame – which allowed doors to shut much more accurately and prevent draughts. Also at that period, the concept of the all-wooden door was replaced by the partially glazed door. It is interesting to note that massive timber doors with strong wrought-ironwork, needed in an age where a door was still required to help resist the occasional attack, were being replaced by doors primarily designed to provide privacy and seclusion.

Chimneys are another house feature of significance. For centuries after the collapse of the Roman Empire, most houses in Britain – and in much of Northern Europe – generally consisted of one large room in which all living was done and everyone was part of the family or community group. The reason was not protection: it was simply the fire. It burned day and night in the middle of the room as the source of heat, the centre of cooking activities and the vital hub around which everything revolved. Its smoke, curing slabs and sides of meat suspended from the rafters, eventually found its way out through the central hole or smoke vent in the roof. Romantic as it may sound, it was far from ideal: everything inside finished up smoke-blackened and, on

windy and stormy days, everyone would be red-eyed and coughing as well.

During the fourteenth century, the chimney was discovered, or·perhaps one should say rediscovered – as the Romans had developed chimneys of sorts when they installed their hypocaust central-heating systems. (Hypocaust heating consisted of a fire or furnace in the basement from which hot gases were ducted under the stone floors of the rooms, keeping them warm – the earliest underfloor or ducted heating system in fact.)

The development of chimneys – and fireplaces – had the most far-reaching effects. It revolutionised house layout and design. No longer did houses have to consist of one room. The family could have as many rooms as they wished and heat them all individually.

The kitchen could, and inevitably did, become a separate domain with a great fireplace solely intended for cooking. Fireplaces in other rooms could be made to suit the room. And of course, the fireplace in the great hall (which was the main room of the house, where most eating and entertaining took place) could be made into a magnificent feature, with coats of arms and heraldic insignia sculpted, carved, painted in some way or emblazoned above it.

Plaish Hall, Shrewsbury is a late Elizabethan gem with brickwork enhanced at corners and around the windows, the exquisite chimneys are also notable.

Externally, houses changed too – with the central smoke vent being replaced by chimneys and houses taking on the recognisable 'chimneys at each end' appearance which every child draws instinctively even today. Coinciding with, or perhaps actively helping, the spread of chimneys was the arrival of the building brick, first brought to Britain by settlers from Flanders in the twelfth or thirteenth centuries and later made in many locations where suitable clay could be found.

Although crudely made and – by modern standards – poorly fired, early bricks proved a successful and durable building material. They were much in demand for building fireplaces, chimneys and chimney stacks in houses in which, because they were wholly of timber construction, they could not otherwise have been built. The arrival of the building brick also produced a new tradesman – the bricklayer – and it is notable that, from the earliest days of building bricks, house designers and bricklayers took great delight in using them to stunning effect. The brickwork on certain Elizabethan chimneys, for instance, still evokes awe and admiration today.

Not that all fireplaces and chimneys were brick-built.

Far from it. Many if not most were built with local stone, as brickmaking and usage stayed largely localised for centuries after their first appearance. Indeed, distant parts of Britain, particularly Scotland and the far West Country, never really took to brick construction. It was only in the Victorian era, when the railways allowed cheap transport of heavy materials over longer distances, that bricks gained the widespread popularity which we now take for granted.

One has also to remember that house-building was for centuries a 'cottage industry' where materials, because of transport difficulties, had to be found as close as possible to the house under construction. In rural areas, it was quite normal for a small quarry to be started nearby to supply the stone for a house – and the reason many country houses and manors have an adjacent pond is because that was where the clay was dug to build it.

This 'local-sourcing' of materials goes further back than that. The Romans built their excellent roads entirely on that principle, excavating small circular quarries on either side of the road they were building as a source of hardcore – rocks and stones – as they advanced.

In this age of global warming and the greenhouse effect, we must not allow ourselves to forget that Britain was once almost as densely wooded as the Amazon basin and that our ancestors depleted our native woodlands over the centuries to build houses, clear land for agriculture and to provide fuel.

The arrival of the chimney and thus the splitting up of houses into separate rooms had another, less desirable, effect. For the first time since the Roman era, society became split into social classes. There would have been a hierarchy and pecking order in households under the old single-room layout, but communal living enforced a clumsy but effective egalitarianism. In a house of many different rooms, certain rooms could have restricted access – thus giving those who had access to them privilege over those who did not.

It seems strange to blame the creation of class distinction on the arrival of the humble chimney. Indeed,

it is possible that the underlying attitudes were already there, and the segregation of households by creating separate rooms merely speeded up a development which might well have evolved anyway. But when one looks at the negative effects over many centuries of the British fixation with class, one might occasionally wish the old central fire and smoke vent in the middle of the roof were still with us!

Paxton, near Berwick, was built by Robert Adam in the latter half of the 18th century and is a lavish, if not-too-big late Palladian mansion, complete with long approach drive and two beautiful symmetrical wings. (Far left)

The library with recessed bookshleves and a roundly-moulded corner – very much an Adam touch – highlighted by this glass case with model ship (Above)

The spectacular drawing room again with the stamp of Robert Adam on it. Intricate plasterwork, furniture made by Chippendale Hay & Co and an endless host of fine details.

THE
DISTANT PAST

E HAVE LOOKED at the social, financial and historical reasons why country houses were built and how those social, financial and historical circumstances changed, causing their decline, decay and destruction. We now need to look at some other aspects and features of the country house that were the main architectural influences on them, why they were built the way they were – and who were the men who had the greatest impact and influence on country house design, layout and setting.

It is not possible within this book to look in depth at the history of European architecture. But a small resume will shed some light on this complex subject and provide clues to the development of country house architecture.

Many architectural styles will be mentioned – such as Romanesque, Gothic, Tudor, Elizabethan and Jacobean, Palladian, Georgian and Gothic Revival (sometimes expressed as Gothick). However, it is very unusual to find a building that is totally of one style.

The reason is that architectural styles very rarely 'arrived' as complete concepts, but often evolved from styles and ideas which had preceded them. Alternatively, architects and builders adopted a new style, but adapted it to suit what was acceptable to the customer, who often wanted features based on existing styles.

Lastly, and this is particularly true of British country houses, architectural ideas would be added to or superimposed on buildings of an earlier style. An existing building would be extended, or would be partly-demolished and 'modernised'. The final result was that many country houses would cheerfully embrace several different styles because of being built at different times.

Also, the philosophy of an architectural style had to be tempered to suit the requirements of a particular building: for instance, Gothic churches and cathedrals bear little or no resemblance to Gothic castles or fortresses – but there are certain common characteristics. We shall see examples of this in later chapters.

It is an axiom of history that future generations will remember earlier civilisations best by their buildings or other durable artefacts. Great buildings, whatever their purpose, inspire awe and convey a sense of immortality which speaks louder than words. A huge impressive stone building lasts for

E mpty and deserted, Ewart Park in Northumberland desperately needs to be rescued before further decay sets in. It is an intriguing example of three different styles, including (left) a castellated Gothic wing and tower. (Left)

P anmure House, near Carnoustie, Tayside. Seat of the Earl of Dalhousie. Rebuilt 1852–1855 in what was called French Renaissance style, this many-turreted extravagance was dynamited in 1955.

Historians and archaeologists surmise that many other considerable civilisations may have grown, flourished and waned in bygone millennia – but they are now totally forgotten because they did not build great, or durable, buildings. They might have evolved fine art, writing, paper and advanced forms of culture and government, but if their buildings and other artefacts were of timber or other biodegradable materials, then they would have disappeared almost without trace. Only stone, and massive quantities of it, endures.

The two great early European civilisations which built in stone or similar durable materials and which have profoundly affected architecture since are those of Greece and Rome. In retrospect, one might say the Greeks were the originators of what we now regard as classical design and vision, whereas the Romans were engineers and organisers who spread the impact of classical design throughout Europe.

Greek architecture has been aptly described as the ideas of timber construction translated into stone – all verticals (columns) and horizontals (entablatures). Roman architecture is much more rounded and plastic, as if it had been formed in moulds. This came in part from the Romans' extensive use and application of cement which could be used not just as mortar but as a very effective outer skin for crude stone, rubble or rough brick.

To the Greeks we owe the ubiquitous four, six or multi-column temple front with entablature and pediment above which even today is regarded as the classic frontage for almost every imposing building that is not starkly modern.

The Romans adopted the Greek pillared or columned front, though often shrinking it to be a simple porch or portico, sometimes with the columns just as decoration on a facade without any structural purpose. The Romans also developed the concept of the larger building built around a central quadrangle or courtyard, or indeed several of these. Their engineering skills also allowed them to design and build structures quite unprecedented in their vision and daring. The most

One of a handful of neglected houses in Humberside which are not so big as to be beyond the scope of a solo restorer, Swanland Hall is a Georgian manor with an interesting extension.

centuries, even thousands of years, but words, once spoken, vanish.

Even in the space and computer age, we stand humbled by the pyramids of Egypt, the temples of the Mayas and the Aztecs, the Minoan ruins at Knossus on Crete, the Coliseum in Rome, the Acropolis at Athens, the temples at Angkor Vat and Pagan or the mausoleum of the Chinese emperor Shihuangdi at Mount Lishan, complete with 6000 buried terracotta soldiers.

Even things which are not entire buildings have their impact on us. Who has not been impressed by the huge ring at Stonehenge or by pictures and film of the giant, gloomily staring heads on Easter Island?

inspired of these was the Pantheon with its huge circular dome, later copied by innumerable architects including, fifteen centuries on, Sir Christopher Wren in his designs for the reconstruction of St Paul's Cathedral.

After the fall of Rome early in the fifth century AD, Europe entered an epoch of cultural decline, conflict and destruction which was to last the better part of a thousand years, a period we generally refer to as the Middle Ages. Although there were many fine individual monarchs who had remarkable castles built, and certain cities developed skilled tradesmen and artisans who produced excellent jewellery, metalware and other artefacts, the general picture throughout Europe was one of poverty, instability, conflict, bloodshed and death.

There were certain kingdoms and empires which prevailed for up to several centuries – such as the triply-misnamed Holy Roman Empire or the dynasties of the Merovingian and Carolingian kings – but the era for the most part was one of fragmentation. Not without reason was it later referred to as the Dark Ages.

Although there were occasional periods of relative peace and stability, life expectancy was exceedingly low, particularly for men. If they did not die in battle or other violence, they could expect to be crippled and killed by disease.

That disease was not necessarily the dreaded scourges such as plague or leprosy, but simple infections made fatal by poor nutrition and sanitation combined with inadequate, often non-existant medical care. In an age of low life expectancy, there was neither the time nor the opportunity to learn skills and crafts which might have led to long-term improvements.

The one body who did have the power, wealth and the central authority to bring about some improvement was the Church, but for centuries it was too corrupt, cleft with intrigue and intent on maintaining its political and secular power to achieve anything. Sad to say, the Church largely made matters worse.

However, the Middle Ages did see the rise of two significant architectural styles, the Romanesque and the Gothic. Because the Church was the one body which had the authority to commission, and the means to pay for, large and significant new buildings, most Romanesque and early Gothic constructions were churches, cathedrals and monasteries. There were strong Gothic influences on the design of certain castles, but most kings and warlords continued to put strength and security above design as priorities for their fortresses.

Another enduring feature of the Middle Ages was the feudal system. Although its introduction and application varied widely from country to country – if one could call the scattered fiefdoms of the time countries – the basic concept was the same. Whereas towns had the population and the resources to build a strong protective wall around them, small villages, hamlets and other scattered rural communities could not afford to build such protection.

So the feudal system evolved whereby the peasants and farmers close to a castle or fortified dwelling paid taxes to the baron or warlord in exchange for protection from attackers or marauders or, in the case of serious warfare, temporary sanctuary inside the castle. The taxes paid were rarely in money, a commodity very few people had in the Middle Ages, but in produce. In England, that became known as the tithe system, whereby everyone gave one tenth of their harvest to the castle. Buildings, known as tithe barns, had to be set up to store such produce.

The system had its faults, but in an age when conflict was rife and bloodshed frequent, it was as good – and as humane – a system as one could hope for. It also established the feudal tradition, where rural dwellers took it for granted that they paid ten per cent of their output, and often provided so many workdays a year, to the local overlord in exchange for protection. However, when such localised warfare eventually waned and all but disappeared, the need for protection diminished. However, the tradition continued and provided the social and economic foundations for the establishment of the country house.

Benholm Castle – a medieval square keep (with a huge crack in the north wall) linked to an eighteenth century Georgian house.

Millearne, near
Auchterader, Perthshire.
Another marvellous Victorian
Gothick house in Perthshire,
complete with arched windows,
stone mullions and transoms
and hundreds of leaded panes.
Demolished 1969. In the East
Gallery, note the beautiful
panelling and plasterwork, and
the wooden archway to the
alcove.

HOPE ON THE HORIZON

THE FIRST POST-Roman architectural style to evolve still bore strong resemblance to its Roman heritage and was subsequently called Romanesque. Introduced to Britain largely as a result of the Norman conquest in 1066, it can be found mainly in early churches and other religious buildings. Among secular constructions, the Tower of London and Windsor Castle are strongly Romanesque.

Of Romanesque manor houses, which one might regard as the early ancestors of the country house, there are very few left and all have been drastically modified over the centuries. Reflecting the continuing need for security at the time of their construction, such manor houses were originally surrounded by moats or by high timber stockades.

Gothic architecture is, with later adaptations of classic Greek and Roman designs, the most enduring architectural style in European history. One would be tempted to assume it came from the Goths, one of the many warring peoples who came and went across the European scene in the last years of the Roman Empire. In fact, the style originated in the twelfth century in the Ile de France, the area north of the River Seine around Paris, and was first called *l'architecture ogivale* – a term still used by some purists today.

The style actually acquired its name retrospectively. Italian architects and artists of the Renaissance derisively called the style 'Gothic' because they regarded it as barbarous and outdated, like the Goths. Ironically, their pejorative expression for the style – and the style itself – have proved to be as enduring as the new Classicism created by its detractors.

The main Gothic characteristics were the use of massive vertical shafts of stonework, regularly spaced, linked by thin infill walls with high, intricate windows with pointed arches, and of high spires and vaulted roofs with long 'ribs' which added to the sense of height. Spires of great height were built, particularly during the aptly-named perpendicular Gothic phase in Britain.

Other Gothic hallmarks were the use of little pinnacles and turrets and the famous 'flying buttresses' which provided structural rigidity against the lateral forces which the high vaulted roofs imposed on the upper masonry of the main stone shafts. Lastly, Gothic is noted for the richness and

Glamis Castle, Tayside, a fine example of original Gothic castle architecture. Historically noted for its spurious links with Macbeth and its more genuine contemporary royal connections. (Left)

Gothic-style entrance gate with crenellated gatehouse at Ripley Castle, Yorks. Note the beautiful pointed archway, the pedestrian gate with dripstone and the trio of tiny lancet windows above the main archway.

complexity of its tracery and decoration, particularly in the 'rayonnant' and 'flamboyant' phases on the Continent.

Gothic architecture reached Britain over the thirteenth and fourteenth centuries, being modified as it came. Much early work was again on churches and other ecclesiastical constructions, though simpler Gothic ideas were applied to castles and fortifications which did not need the ornate complexity of the church designs. Hampton Court, Glamis Castle, Conway and Caernarvon Castles and Penshurst Place in Kent are among the enduring original Gothic secular buildings built in Britain.

It is worth remembering about this era that there were relatively few 'public' buildings. Castles, towers and fortresses were built for the mighty, chapels and monasteries built for the Church. However, because of the scourges of poverty, early death and the constant risk of one's house being attacked, and possibly pillaged and burned, few durable houses were built by private individuals.

Under the Tudors – particularly Henry VIII – there were two significant developments. One was the creation of what we might now call stronger central government, in the shape of a more powerful monarchy, which gradually prevailed over the powers of regional and local nobles. The other was the dissolution of the monasteries – Henry's revenge on the Roman Catholic Church for not granting him a divorce. In many respects, the dissolution and subsequent destruction of nearly 800 monasteries was an act of political barbarism which destroyed irreplaceable buildings, manuscripts and art

treasures, and which wrongly brought millions of pounds' worth of gold and jewellery into the royal coffers.

But two beneficial results flowed from the Tudor actions. One was to create stability and a measure of longer-term peace for large areas of Britain, particularly in England. The other was to break the old power of the Church and ensure that wealth which in previous times would have gone to monasteries and the churches now stayed in the hands of individuals and secular bodies.

The former allowed the freer development of activities like trade and shopkeeping, travel, inns and public houses. The latter contributed to the creation of personal, private wealth. One thing which so many political theorists overlook, even today, is that true wealth is accumulative – it takes a lifetime, even several lifetimes, to build up a big, enduring family business or estate. There are examples – mainly during the last hundred years – when great fortunes have been made overnight, but they are the exception. In most instances enduring wealth has been slowly and meticulously accumulated.

One of the manifestations of such accumulating wealth was the growth, perhaps even proliferation, of the manor house in Tudor times. Although it had been in existence for centuries, it really came in to its own in the sixteenth century. It, too, was linked to land ownership, though on a more modest scale. But the manor house and the castle, now more inclined towards gracious living than pure defence, provided the parentage for the great country houses which were to come.

Haden Hill Hall, West Midlands is a Tudor House (right) with what appears to be a Victorian extension in a Jacobean style.

A NEW DAWN

HE MANOR HOUSE, although originally moated or stockaded, became gradually less protected as the threat of conflict diminished. It was sometimes built of stone, in areas where it was plentiful and close by, but more often it was built of wood with the spaces between the main timbers infilled with mud, mortar or brick. Manor houses would be U- or H-shaped or, most frequently, E-shaped with a courtyard created by the wings. The entrance was almost always in the centre of the back wall of the courtyard.

In fact, so-called E-shaped houses were often just U-shaped with a small entrance porch, topped by an overhanging dormer-type window and gable, forming the middle stroke of the E.

This entrance led directly into the main hall, which was the key room of the house: guests were entertained there, meals served and eaten there, everything except sleeping happened there. It was, in fact, the remnant of the old single-room house with the central fire. Other rooms were now in the wings.

Early Tudor and Elizabethan manor houses had a characteristic which is unique among British dwellings, though not uncommon overseas. The walls and their finishes were the same outside and in. The timbers – usually massive oak – were left exposed to dry, weather and darken naturally over the decades. The gaps were filled in with 'wattle and daub' – mud plastered over and finished with a white or tinted wash. Relatively few of these houses now survive – but one which is being restored with total attention to detail and no expense spared is Sinai Park, overlooking Burton upon Trent.

Roofs of such houses were covered according to whatever materials were locally available, and ranged from thin stone slabs to fired tiles to thatch. Internal floors mostly would be flagstones on the ground floor and in the cellars with wooden floors upstairs. Windows, as mentioned earlier, would be of small glass panes held by tiny hoops of metal wire on to lead frames and fixed rigidly in position.

Another characteristic of the timber Tudor and Elizabethan manor house was the 'overhang' – the upper floor was frequently bigger than the ground floor. Various reasons have been advanced for this quirk, none of which is wholly satisfactory. They include the idea that houses in towns, where the streets were very narrow, were built to gain more living space without encroaching on the street, so the overhang was developed. Others say it was a way of preventing rainwater, dripping off the roof or down the walls, from soaking into the bottom timbers and causing rot. Whatever the reason, it has proved an enduringly visible idiosyncrasy of the era.

Although manor houses were built less and less with defence in mind, many retained some defensive features – as this moated manor house near Batley in Yorkshire shows. (Left)

An H-shape hall, Lancashire. A fine remaining example of a timber, wattle and daub Elizabethan manor house.

The overhang also led to one characteristic component of the early manor house – the dragon beam, a massive, slightly curved horizontal timber which ran out diagonally to the corners and acted as a cantilever to hold the great weight otherwise pressing down into thin air.

Manor houses of that period had a proliferation of gables and complicated roofs which were all carefully designed to channel rainwater into valleys and gullies. These in turn emptied the rainwater into lead gutters – another significant development of the era – which were drained by square leaden downpipes, often with exquisite detailing and ornamentation. These in turn fed the rainwater into large butts and barrels.

Why? Because rainwater was then a very valuable commodity. For certain houses, it was the primary source of fresh water, and not a drop was to be wasted. The alternative was fetching water from a distant stream or well. We now know the hazards of drinking water channelled along leaden gutters and downpipes – but in those days no such worries prevailed. There were far too many other health hazards – such as hunger and thirst – which were considered more compelling to treat in the circumstances.

Another significant aspect of manor houses was the growth of decoration, in part to conceal the bareness of inner walls, which often deteriorated quickly through dampness and smoke-blackening, but also because decoration has always been the first aspiration once immediate living requirements are fulfilled. Wood panelling, which allowed the use of varnishes and stains, carving and bas-relief, became the main medium of interior decoration – and some of the carving, panelling and strapwork of the era has yet to be surpassed.

The predominant features of the Tudor and Elizabethan manor houses were, therefore, the U, E or H-shape, allowing the creation of attractive courtyards, and the proliferation of small gables, even on quite long facades. In the north of England and in poorer areas, timber construction was more prevalent, but in areas where stone was available, or where bricks could be fired from locally abundant clay, either of these was used.

Although individual windows were small because of glaziers' inability to make glass into large sheets, architects and designers overcame this limitation by designing larger-appearing windows which were split into smaller 'lights' by mullions (vertical stone bars) and transoms (horizontal stone bars), often to brilliant effect. Mullions and transoms were almost always chamfered or scalloped to improve appearance and to increase the amount of vision at an angle through the window. It is also possible that chamfering of transoms helped to drain away rainwater.

An interesting house of the early eighteenth or possibly late seventeenth century. Annesley Hall, Nottinghamshire is still an H-plan but shows design details of classical or Georgian influence.

Although manor houses were less and less built with defence in mind, there were many which retained defensive features. As mentioned earlier, some had moats or stockades – though increasingly these were houses built on earlier sites which already had one or the other. Those built on new sites more often than not did without. Others were built with strong external walls with a few tiny windows looking out but, around the enclosed inner courtyard, all the more civilised features of Tudor and Elizabethan living visible. Access to the courtyard was gained through a guarded gatehouse which, in certain instances, could be a very imposing edifice.

One building which showed these developments very well, and was a building of unparalleled splendour in its time, was the palace of Nonsuch. Built by Henry VIII near Ewell on the south-west approaches to London from riches plundered from the monasteries, it was meant to rival the palaces and chateaux of the French monarchy, particularly Fontainebleau. It showed Tudor architecture at its most magnificent and was surrounded by acres of meticulously laid-out formal gardens. Started in 1538 and virtually completed before Henry's death, it sadly was never put to proper use. Sold to one of Cromwell's generals after the Civil War, it was returned to the monarchy in 1660. A decade later, Charles II foolishly gave it to Lady Castlemaine, one of his most unscrupulous mistresses, who decided to demolish it in 1682 to save on upkeep costs. No trace of it now remains. As a footnote, it is worth commenting that Nonsuch, like Hampton Court and other royal residences, was located in a rural area away from London: such royal emphasis on country living may have set a trend, but it is more likely it was a reflection of already prevalent aristocratic attitudes towards living in the country.

Without doubt, the Tudor and Elizabethan periods

Ledston Hall, near Leeds has a complete yet complicated symmetry. The 'Holburn gables' with alternating pediments and 'oeil de boeuf' windows in them form a very ornate overall impression.

in England demonstrated a perceptible shift away from defence towards gracious living and the architecture and interior decoration of the times reflected this.

The architecture of the period had three other noteworthy characteristics. First, it still showed occasional touches of gothic – the odd pointed archway or vault, or the use of Gothic-style battlements and spires if the requirements of the building called for them.

Royal palaces aside, second, it was an architecture largely conceived and built by local tradesmen, who were practical men with few overblown ideas and who built to a human scale. No need for nine or ten-foot ceilings in rooms other than the great hall if the average person stood five foot six.

Third, a house was rarely built to some elaborately conceived plan. It was built or extended as and when the house owner had money, and the west wing might well have been built by a different set of tradesmen with other ideas from those who built the gate-house. This helps account for some Tudor houses with widely differing windows and gables on a single frontage.

Most importantly, Tudor and Elizabethan architecture was very much a British, or perhaps English, style. It was unique to these islands and evolved here in relative isolation, well away from the neo-Classical, post-Renaissance architecture which was evolving in Italy and would gradually spread to France and the rest of continental Europe. But increasing cross-Channel trade and travel were to bring these influences to Britain, and to effect a profound change on the country house.

Before the neo-Classical arrived, something else did, and from an unexpected quarter. An under-appreciated aspect of British history is the great influence Holland and the Low Countries have had on these islands. We tend to remember best the impact of those peoples or nations – the Romans, the Vikings, the Normans – who occupied or settled in these islands through force of arms. The influence of the Dutch, with whom we have had centuries of good relations and trade virtually unblemished by war, we sadly forget. But the Dutch have

had great impact on British house design at certain points in history – and certainly had so in the early and mid-seventeenth century.

That was the period when Jacobean architecture gradually supplanted Elizabethan. In many ways the two styles had much in common, particularly in the extensive use of dark, ornate wood panelling for internal decoration. However, what became known as the Jacobean style owed much to the civic architecture of wealthy Amsterdam and other Dutch trading cities.

The wooden-framed window made its first appearance and houses gained steeper, more visible roofs. But the most striking feature of the Jacobean era was the very ornate multiple gable, lavishly decorated. This became very popular, as did a lot of other external decoration. But, behind these enhanced facades, the basic design and concept of country and manor houses had changed relatively little. The really big change was about to come.

I slay House: Regarded as the finest house in the southern Hebrides, it is a classically austere Scots mansion lying at the head of Lochindaal. Rumoured to be a not infrequent guest is Mrs Margaret Thatcher . . . Inside, a dizzying downward view of the house's magnificent spiral staircase.

RENAISSANCE
AND
REFORMATION

HERE ARE TWO similar words describing the two most important and far-reaching developments in Europe which brought the Middle Ages to a close. They are the Renaissance and the Reformation. The two are separate and superficially unconnected – but they have a strong link and, in combination, have had a huge cumulative effect on subsequent European history. In essence, both were reactions against the power of the Church – though one movement was largely secular, the other profoundly religious.

As mentioned earlier, during the Middle Ages the Church had become an extraordinarily corrupt institution whose influence penetrated almost every aspect of life – almost as the state has done in certain totalitarian states in the twentieth Century.

It seems laughable now, but the influence of the Church was so total it had an utterly stultifying effect on human activity. The main thrust of Christian belief, as expressed in those days, was that humans were sinful, imperfect creatures riven by wrongful lusts and passions and only by a life of penance and suffering could people redeem themselves sufficiently to be considered worthy to gain access after death to the Kingdom of God.

(Funnily enough, it is a belief which re-emerged very strongly in Britain during the eighteenth and nineteenth centuries – and it is perhaps no coincidence that its re-emergence coincided with a spectacular renewed interest in Gothic architecture).

Penance might take many forms, but whatever form it took, it could – and did – involve making donations to the Church – of money, goods, food. But however much one tried to achieve, it was never enough. One always fell short, or transgressed again, or failed in one tiny but crucial detail. People spent a lifetime in thrall to the Church and gave an absurd share of their meagre earnings to it. Doubtless, there were many men in the Church with high ideals, who were not corrupt, but the whole body was badly debased, and became more so the further up the hierarchy one penetrated.

The hold and influence of the Church was so total it became an insurmountable obstacle to

Pillars of society . . . A house party at an unidentified Scottish country house pose confidently for the camera, probably at about the turn of the century. The gamekeeper's dog was obviously unable to hold still long enough for the slow shutter speed. (Left)

Riccarton House, near Currie, Lothian. Dating from three periods – the 14th century, 1621 and 1827 – its stonework was eventually attacked by smoke pollution. Demolished 1956.

The great Palladian masterpiece of James Paine, Nostell Priory stands not far from Wakefield, Yorkshire. On the far right is the later addition by Robert Adam – the only part of the building to have pillars rather than pilasters. (Above)

Minto House, Borders. Unique L-shaped house near Denholm with more than 80 rooms and an amazing central staircase. Used as a school in its final years (hence the fire escape on the right), it was demolished in 1974. (Right)

Ladykirk House, near Norham, Berwickshire. Gorgeous Georgian mansion with long, low wings (demolished before the picture was taken) overlooking the Tweed. The remainder of the building was lost in 1967. (Middle)

Nostell Priory's main building, a close up showing the pilasters – shallow pseudo-columns or piers projecting from the walls, they were often used to create the visual effect of a portico without having to build one. (Far right)

66

Blythswood – beautiful Victorian villa in Palladian-Georgian style lying between the Rivers Clyde and Casto, it was demolished in 1929.

progress. People either joined it or submitted to it. The Church had effective control over almost every aspect of human life which feudal overlords did not have already. Its influence reached great heights of absurdity. For instance, for centuries artists were only allowed to paint one subject – that of the Madonna and Child. No landscapes, no still lifes, no domestic or other current images, no scenes of nature, no nudes, no biblical scenes even.

Even then there were strict guidelines: the Virgin Mary could not be portrayed as voluptuous; she had to be totally demure and pristine. Christ could not be shown as a normal child – with spots, a runny nose or the chubby wrinkles of babyhood. He had to be a kind of instant perfect miniature adult. It is hardly surprising that, faced with that level of artistic censorship, the art of the Middle Ages is limited and, to some people, dull. Tragically, it also means it is an era of which we have virtually no pictorial records.

The Renaissance – literally 'rebirth' – started in Italy as a movement against the artistic restrictions enforced by the church and which harked back to the halcyon days of Greece and Rome, the 'classical times' of learning and freedom and open pursuit of knowledge. Just what was the spark which set the new fire going we do not know, but it showed its first glimmerings in the thirteenth century and evolved from there.

The Reformation we can date more accurately.

Martin Luther issued his ninety-five theses on 31 October 1517. Essentially, he and many other thinking churchmen were appalled at the corruption of the Church and wanted to cleanse and revitalise it from within. But the strong and implacable reaction to his ideas from the Church eventually 'forced him into opposition'.

The efforts of Luther and other reform-minded churchmen – such as Zwingli, Calvin and Knox – eventually led to the creation of the Protestant churches. Their influence spread through much of Northern Europe and caused such panic in the Roman Catholic Church that a counter-Reformation movement was established, the most notorious, if unintended feature of

Roseneath, Gareloch, Dumbartonshire. One of the seats of the Dukes of Argyll, it was an Italian-style gem built in 1803. Churchill, Montgomery and Eisenhower are said to have planned D-Day there. It was dynamited in 1961.

which, was the Inquisition. The counter-Reformation had greatest impact in Italy and Spain, which remain today the two predominant Roman Catholic nations of Europe.

Again, we could shrug these matters aside as footnotes of history, but the long-term impact of both movements simply cannot be underestimated. In Britain alone, the troubles in Northern Ireland, the Jacobite rebellion and many constitutional facets of the British monarchy are linked to consequences of the Reformation and all that flowed from it.

Both movements were to influence the country house, though here the Renaissance was to play by far the greater role.

Largely thanks to the Renaissance, the city-states of Italy in the fifteenth and sixteenth centuries were seedbeds for considerable growth and prosperity. Nobles, merchants and professional men accumulated wealth and set out to build fine homes reflecting that wealth. At the same time, the new artistic freedoms of the era brought many talented artists, craftsmen, designers and architects to the fore. It proved a spectacularly successful combination. For the first time since the Roman Empire there was creative and unfettered human talent available – and the wealth to transform their ideas into reality for secular, personal and civic purposes rather than for military or religious ones.

The results transformed Italy. A profusion of fine villas and public buildings were built in what we would now call neo-Classical style. Frontages and porticos with columns and pediments, courtyards and terraced gardens, magnificent front steps and a proliferation of marble statues and fountains, contributed to a magnificence unseen since the heyday of Rome.

Walls were mostly smooth stucco – plasterwork – or tinted 'Roman cement' with abundant use of marble, ceramic tiling, mosaic and other smooth finishes on floors, staircases and terraces. This lavish use of fine smooth stucco opened up new possibilities of interior decoration. One could employ artists to paint great and spectacular works of art on the walls and ceilings. Great friezes and frescoes were conceived and executed, some of which took years to complete.

The era spawned dozens of fine architects – most of whom were the self-taught sons of builders and masons – and arguably the greatest trio of near-contemporary painters the world has ever known – da Vinci, Michaelangelo and Raphael. It also produced the man who, although not universally regarded as the greatest architect of all time, is certainly the most influential – Andrea Palladio. From whose name we get the word Palladianism.

His influence stems not just from the quality and

beauty of his buildings – the most famous of which is the Villa Rotonda near Venice – but from his published books, including his historic *Quattro Libri dell'Architettura*, which expressed in book form what he regarded as the classic laws of proportion, good design, decoration and enhancement. It became virtually a 'Bible' for entire later generations of architects. Through the influence of Benjamin Latrobe, a British architect who emigrated to America, the early civic architecture of the United States was, if not strictly Palladian, then most distinctly neo-Classical.

Word of the splendour of Renaissance Italy spread – not at the speed it would do nowadays, but it spread.

Those few people in other countries who had the money and opportunity to travel went to Italy. Among them were members of the British nobility and aristocracy, who returned home dazzled by the neo-Classical Eden they had seen and determined to create an even better one at home.

The initial problem was that relatively few British builders or architects had visited Italy, but a man who did manage to go was one Inigo Jones. He and those who followed in his footsteps were to recreate the full splendour of the Italian Renaissance, or by now post-Renaissance, in Britain.

S econd on the right of Newburgh's frontage is a 'classic' late eighteenth century facade, then to the left an Elizabethan facade followed finally on the far left by a rather nondescript, possibly nineteenth century section with a hipped and slated roof.

THE ZENITH

HE IMPACT ON Britain of Inigo Jones and the neo-Classical, Palladian and Baroque architects who followed in his footsteps cannot be underestimated. To draw a modern culinary analogy, it would be like the impact of Chinese, Indian or other oriental food on an individual whose tastes since birth had been shaped by the local fish and chip shop. It might be an excellent fish-and-chip shop – just as Tudor, Elizabethan and Jacobean architecture had much to commend it – but the vision and scope of the new architecture was far beyond what had gone before it.

It should be said that Inigo Jones had predecessors, but he enjoyed the double blessing of having undoubted genius and royal patronage. Born less than a decade after Shakespeare in 1573, the son of a London clothworker, he visited Italy as early as 1603, giving his then occupation as a picture-maker. After his return to Britain, he worked at court as the designer of stage sets and costumes for the great *bals masques* then much in vogue. His designs were streets ahead of the times and his ability to sketch vivid lines and colours at high speed was almost unprecedented.

He returned to Italy in 1613, stayed for a year and a half and returned bedazzled by the work of Palladio and Scamozzi – he met the latter in Venice. In 1615, he was appointed Surveyor of the King's Works and held the post until the Civil War in 1642. During those twenty-seven years, he designed several royal palaces and other buildings, all of which were utterly different from the Jacobean designs which were then the norm.

Architectural historians point out that Inigo Jones' genius was his ability to adapt Palladian designs and add new ideas which somehow made his work distinctly English. He is best remembered for three buildings – the Queen's House at Greenwich (started 1616, but only completed between 1629 and 1635), the Prince's Lodging at Newmarket (1619–22, alas now destroyed) and the Banqueting House in Whitehall, London (1619–22), which is the sole remaining vestige of the great Whitehall Palace which burned down in a massive fire in 1698.

Fire destroyed another of Inigo Jones' greatest creations – the great classical portico of old St Paul's Cathedral, all fourteen huge columns and two pilasters of which were devoured by the Great Fire of London in 1666. The portico was an architectural *tour de force* in more ways than one: he managed to add a totally Classical facade to a wholly Gothic structure so the one complemented rather than detracted from the other. And Sir Christopher Wren, in his designs for the replacement St Paul's, which still stands today, kept more than a hint of Inigo Jones' design in the portico of the new

V ista and vision . . . the setting of a country house was frequently as important, if not more so, than the house itself. House, lawns, gardens, trees and water were intended to blend into an eye-rivetting picture – epitomised by Scotland's Keith House. (Left)

H awkshead House, near Paisley, Renfrewshire. Seat of the Ross family, the house was enlarged and improved in 1782. Used from early this century as a mental hospital, it was demolished in 1955.

structure.

Although Inigo Jones and others brought the concepts and design ideas of post-Renaissance Italy to Britain in the early seventeenth century, it was only after Cromwell's death and the return of the monarchy in the 1650s that the great flowering of English culture, linked to the Restoration, began. With it came the start of the long golden age of the country house.

It is impossible to do justice in the space of this book to the many architects, designers, craftsmen, decorators and landscape architects whose talents were to elevate the English, eventually the British, country house to the creative pinnacles of the following 200 years – though a sampling of the more notable great names is to be found in the chapter, 'Great Builders'. However, it is possible to outline some of the main new ideas and concepts which were to affect and influence country house design.

Up to and including the Jacobean era, most manor houses and mansions, as previously noted, were still laid out in E, H or U-shape, or were set out like a squared 'O' around a courtyard or figure '8' around two courtyards. But the depth of any one wing or block was rarely more than one room, at most two. The facades might be very impressive, but if one were to penetrate a facade, it would not be much more than twenty or thirty feet – or at most the length of a trimmed tree trunk – before one reached the far wall and was out in the fresh air again.

It was rare, too, in Elizabethan or Jacobean houses to find corridors or long hallways. The designs purposely had one room leading to another to a third or even forth, usually with strong lockable doors between each room. This was for defence. Although the days of moats, drawbridges, portcullises and clockwise spiral staircases (so the defenders had more room to work their sword arms) were now gone, there were still occasions when unwelcome visitors with lethal intentions might intrude. Inter-connecting rooms with lockable doors allowed better defence than corridors.

But the neo-Classical designs could include such then novel concepts as corridors. That meant a building could

*M*ilnsbridge Hall, *Huddersfield fascinating in its absurdity. The huge pediment with 'oculus' evidently has nothing behind it, the side wings which continue the slope of the pediment are another oddity.*

be at least two rooms and a wide hallway deep from external wall to external wall. Another new feature, particularly of Palladianism, was the rotunda. This was a central rounded tower or canopy, wholly or partly-glazed, above a great hall and stairway in the centre of the house. Thanks to daylight coming in through the rotunda, this area could be made quite magnificent rather than the gloomy ill-lit central lobby it would have been without it.

If the design of the house did not run to a rotunda – which was a costly item and difficult to make totally waterproof – an attractive alternative was a Venetian or Serliana window either above the front door or at the head of the stairs. This was a three-part window framed by four classical columns or pilasters. Left and right windows were the same size, topped by flat entablatures which also acted as lintels to carry the masonry above. The centre window was wider and higher, with an arched top. The sum total is most impressive and is one of the many great hallmarks of a Palladian house.

Another external hallmark of Palladianism is the great central pediment above a portico, often the full height of the building. This portico may vary in prominence from being twenty or thirty feet deep to very shallow, with the pilasters merged into the main walls.

Andrea Palladio himself emphasised a belief in strict proportions between height and width, distances between windows and other apertures, and believed in clean, smooth external surfaces – stucco or 'Roman cement' with white or pale pastel colours – and neat, uncluttered pediments and surrounds for external doors and windows.

However, like all successful simple – or apparently simply – formulae, no one could leave it alone. Each successive group and generation of architects, while nodding briefly to the master, sought to add their special stamp to the basic formula. In most instances, it meant additions rather than subtractions. Pediments (always the most instantly visible feature, just as the gables were on Elizabethan and Jacobean houses) became more and more ornate, with oculus windows, great cornices with dentils, elaborately decorated entablatures and huge bas-relief heraldic figures carved in the tympanum.

The corners of houses were enhanced by massive quoins; arches were topped by complex carved keystones; quoins became the norm around doors and windows; bull-faced masonry replaced the smooth uncluttered walls the old master called for. Eventually, the apex of pediments disappeared and the so-called broken pediment became the norm. Great parapets or balustrades topped the walls and once-simple hipped roofs were replaced by a phantasmagoria of complex towers and rooflines of every description.

However, for all their pomp and complexity, the ancestry and heredity of these structures could still be identified. In basic concept, they were the descendants of the neo-Classical buildings first evolved and built in Italy. Their roots were utterly different from the Early English Gothic, Elizabethan and Jacobean houses which had been the norm in Britain until then.

The most ornate of these 'classical' houses were labelled English Baroque, as they were often copied from, or inspired by, Baroque buildings on the Continent. Probably the two best-known baroque houses in Britain are Blenheim, near Woodstock, Oxfordshire, built for the Duke of Marlborough, and Castle Howard, Yorkshire. Over the years, however, we have come to call most British houses of that era 'Georgian' – be they neo-Classical, Palladian or Baroque – as their heydey coincided with the reign of the four Hanoverian Kings of that name.

The effect of these 'Georgian' designs was to allow houses to have many more rooms and to change, indeed end, the role of the traditional central main hall. True, one still entered the house into a big hall, but it became purely a reception area. It was designed to impress, indeed overawe, but it was no longer the place where the host received and entertained his guests, especially not when there was a plethora of fine new rooms to choose from – morning room, study, library, coffee room and so on.

There might well be, indeed there almost always was, a great room for the big social functions which were becoming more and more part of the annual calendar of the country house. But it would be placed some way from the entrance hall, reached by various rooms of ascending magnificence. In most cases, too, the great room or hall would look out on to the terraced gardens or the park, which guests were eventually able to reach directly through that most coveted of installations, French windows.

Indeed, the splendour of the gardens and parkland in which they were set allowed the great British country houses eventually to match or outshine the best and greatest of the continental palazzos and chateaux. Here there were two severely opposed schools of thought. One was embodied by the great French *createur de jardins* and

Just west of Dundee lies the House of Gray, it is an austere symmetrical mansion with simple central pediment and French-style towers. Although it has been abandoned for many years it is now being restored.

A classic example of a big house with a beautiful pedimental main facade, yet the rest of Walsingham Abbey and House in Norfolk is very dull and dreary.

landscape archtitect, Andre le Notre, the other by the inimitable and indomitable 'Capability' Brown. While it is difficult to itemise all the differences in approach the two had, one can describe the two approaches in a nutshell.

Andre le Notre created gardens as if they were extensions of the ornate buildings they surrounded, exquisitely composed and laid out in perfect and detailed symmetry with immaculate paths, low hedges and flower beds, bringing nature into the shapes of architecture. Capability Brown, mainly using the three materials of lawn, serpentine lakes of smooth water and slim deciduous trees, tried to make gardens and parkland look as if nature had created them that way, even if thousands of man-hours had gone into creating that illusion.

While the richest families were able to recruit the brightest and best of the new architects and meet the often incredible costs of building their Classical, Palladian or Baroque houses, those with more modest means did the next best thing – they put a modern (for the era) facade on an existing house. Some of these were very successful, others went woefully astray. Indeed,

there are some houses in Britain which have become 'all things to all men' over the centuries, with three or four different facades, each from a different era and thus a different style.

But the British, it must be conceded, are innately conservative and, during the last quarter of the eighteenth century, a strong neo-Gothic movement sprang up, whose influence was to last throughout the Victorian era. It was a movement peculiar to Britain, and virtually no other country took it up. It is difficult to explain how it arose, other than to say that Britain, more than most other nations, has always been torn between a desire for the 'good life' and a strong sense of puritan guilt for indulging in it.

The effects of this have left their mark on our history. The Civil War and the conflict between Cavaliers and Roundheads is one example. The rise of John Wesley and the Methodist Church was another. The historic see-sawing between great sexual openness (notably in Shakespeare's day, during the Restoration and since the 1960s) is matched by times of great public sexual repression – which reached absurd proportions during the Victorian era.

Less obvious but just as significant, certain other cultural developments went hand in hand. The upper-class bawdy Restoration comedies of Sheridan, Congreve and Wytcherley, for instance, paralleled the arrival of the new architecture from Italy. A century later, however, there was a strong counter-movement towards the romantic, the mystic, the terrifying, the unknown. This was to spawn the 'Gothic novel', usually set in strange and as yet unexplored foreign lands or in some grim, ghastly country house full of weird nocturnal noises and unnamed terrors.

The demand for Gothic novels was matched by a demand, by those who could indulge in such whims, for Gothic houses. The two most notable of these were Strawberry Hill and Fonthill Abbey.

Strawberry Hill was, appropriately, built for the Gothic writer Horace Walpole and gave rise to the expression 'Strawberry Hill Gothic'. Fonthill Abbey is briefly mentioned in the portrait of Sheffield Park as the ultimate extravagance and folly of a tragi-comic figure called William Beckford. It looked like a vast medieval abbey and proved the downfall of both Beckford and its architect, James Wyatt.

However, one should not decry the neo-Gothic era. Some of the most astounding and beautiful country houses fall into the Gothic domain. They are also among the country houses which have suffered most grievously during the epoch of destruction. There are various reasons for this: many were among the last to be built and belonged to people whose fortunes were most at risk. Also, many were built very cheaply and nastily – all facade and no core. That meant they let in water quickest, and fell prey to the demon rots more quickly too.

Many of the finest neo-Gothic houses were built in Scotland, especially in Perthshire. They were built as extravagant hunting lodges for the *nouveau-riches* of the Victorian era and, when bad times and high rates really hit home – mostly in the years after the Second World War – the bulldozer and crane-ball then seemed the only feasible cure. Also, as there were so many other neo-Gothic piles still standing, few people raised much protest when the destruction took place.

It is often difficult to specify when the neo-Gothic stopped and Victorian architecture started. One would have to say that the one really ran into the other. Also, the Victorians were able to indulge in a great panoply of architectural styles, ranging from the utterly simple to the most outrageously complex.

To take three examples in one London Street – it is remarkable, indeed incredible, that King's Cross, St Pancras and the old Euston stations were built within a few years of each other. King's Cross is simple, almost rustic Italian, unpretentious to the point of austerity. Euston was neo-Classical with ponderous Victorian overtones with its famous triumphal arch. St Pancras is the railway's answer to Neuschwanstein – the ultimate

pinnacle of Gothic phantasmagoria. Yet all could qualify for the adjective Victorian.

One has also to remember that the Victorian era was the first and foremost age of building on a massive scale – of factories, warehouses, offices, railway stations and great urban sprawls. Architects were no longer dependent on, nor did they actively seek, commissions to build country houses. The commissions were most gratifying to receive when they did come, but there were too many other tasks awaiting their attentions first. Whereas, a century earlier, to design a great country house was probably the pinnacle of an architect's aspirations, now he might want to build a great terminal station for one of the railway companies or a huge hotel at one of the spas for the growing holiday trade.

That in itself indicates how, within one or two generations, the emphasis and demographic weight of Britain had shifted. As said in an earlier chapter, Britain went from being a rural to an urban society within one or two generations – and that, more than anything else, contributed to the decline of the country house.

Guisachan House, Tomich, Invernesshire: Arguably the most isolated stately home in Britain, it was built in the 19th century in a glen beside Glen Affric. Sold early this century and de-roofed, it is now a gaunt shell.

*K*inkeil: Described in a bygone gazetteer as 'an ancient baronial tower belonging to the MacKenzies of Gairloch', it has in recent years been made into a fine modern residence, one of the best in Easter Ross. The interior of white, roughcast plaster, wooden ceilings and stone-flagged floors shows how the simplest of decor and finish can be made effective and luxurious.

A GRIM TOLL

T WOULD BE both a challenge and a privilege to record in detail every country house destroyed in the past 120 years, but the space and scope of this book do not allow for that. We can but look at the figures, pick out the counties hardest hit and select some of the countless lost names for especial mention. We can also be grateful that, thanks to the Victoria and Albert Museum exhibition of 1974 and the subsequently published book, *The Destruction of the Country House*, the alarm bells were finally rung and the slaughter-by-bulldozer brought to a stop.

However, we should not think that all is now well. There are nearly 200 houses still endangered in Britain, many because of the obstinacy or pride of owners who have not got the money to save them but cannot bring themselves to sell to someone who has. There are many cases, too, of houses in the possession of local authorities who cannot, in the current climate of strict Whitehall supervision of much local authority spending, do anything other than limit vandalism and try to find a buyer.

All in all, another 100 country houses may not see the twentieth century out, even though it is estimated that for the first time there may be more buyers ready to take on the restoration of a country house than there are derelict country houses available.

Looking back over the dark years of destruction, there is not a county in England which cannot number five to ten country houses lost. Many have lost far more. Wales and Scotland have lost 400 apiece and the figures for Ireland – where destruction currently continues at a frightening rate – have yet to be compiled.

In England, ten counties including Berkshire, Derbyshire, Hampshire and Herefordshire have each lost twenty houses. Norfolk has lost almost thirty; Essex twenty-eight; Staffordshire thirty; Suffolk thirty-seven; Lincolnshire forty-two; Kent forty-five. Northern losses are frightening – fifty-five to sixty lost in Lancashire and a devastating seventy or more demolished in Yorkshire.

Scotland's death toll goes on and on. The worst-hit counties are Angus, Fife and what was Midlothian – with twenty-five apiece – with Perthshire lamenting the loss of thirty, now possibly more, and Aberdeenshire thirty-seven.

Not that every house lost was an irreplaceable gem. Some were grim, ugly places designed by third-rate architects, poorly built and badly maintained virtually since completion. But they were so beautiful, so idiosyncratic, that they still exercise a hold on us, even as sepia prints in old books. How,

Unfortunately the alarm bells which rang after the Victoria and Albert Museum's exhibition in 1974, about the destruction of the country house, were too late for the demolished Knoll's House, Salford. (Left)

Gordon Castle, Morayshire. One of the seats of the Dukes of Richmond and Gordon, a huge but architecturally bland palace beside the River Spey. One facade was an incredible 568 foot long. Demolished in 1955.

Alder House, Lancashire, a delightful 1697 house with many classic Northern traits, numerous gables and strongly accentuated dripstones – suited to an area of heavy rainfall – among them.

the question wells up again and again, could we have allowed them to be destroyed?

There was the immaculate splendour of Frampton Court in Dorset, built in 1740 on the site of an old priory. Enlarged during the nineteenth Century, it became the seat of the Sheridans until, needing countless repairs, it was demolished in 1935. Or the fascinating Fremnells in Essex, first built in the sixteenth century but with a magnificent Jacobean frontage added in 1640. Regarded by architectural historians as one of the finest houses of its period, it was submerged around 1955 in the new Hanningfield reservoir.

A great loss to Cornwall and the West Country was Bosahan House, long the seat of the Vivians. It was a picture-postcard dreamy country house with manicured lawns contrasting with honeysuckle and other creepers rioting across the weathered stone walls. Too much decay and too few funds led to its demolition in 1965.

Among the dozen and more fine houses demolished in County Durham, Coxhoe Hall went almost unnoticed

and unlamented. A gloomy, slab-faced seventeenth century mansion, it fell into ever-greater disrepair, was used briefly by the Army in the Second World War and was demolished in 1955. No great loss? Well, Elizabeth Barrett Browning was born there ...

Some houses were demolished because they were simply too big to be viable. Eaton Hall in Cheshire, built for the Dukes of Westminster in 1870, was demolished during the 1960s because it was a Victorian Gothic extravagance with which later generations of Westminsters didn't know what to do. The new Eaton Hall is Britain's only ultra-modern stately home – though there have been rumours it may come down to make way for something more orthodox.

A similar fate befell Douglas Castle in Lanarkshire in 1939. A vast, ugly pseudo-fortress with dozens of Gothic-arched windows, it was in fact only one eighth of the size first proposed for the edifice. However, the Douglas-Homes preferred the comforts of The Hirsel, their border seat, and gave up Douglas. The new M74 Carlisle-Glasgow motorway now bisects the estate on which the castle once stood.

All too many country houses fell prey to fire, and not all blazes were accidental. Whatever caused them, some of the conflagrations helped solve the knotty problem of what to do with the abandoned place. Significantly, very few if any country houses were rebuilt after the flames. Among the dozens ravaged by fire were Penicuik House in Midlothian (1899), Lincolnshire's Uffington House (1904), the magnificent Stoke Edith in Herefordshire (1927), Suffolk's delightful Assington Hall (1957) and the small but enchanting Aldbar Castle in Angus (1964).

Two which are, however, destined for restoration after fire are High Head in Cumbria and Sir John Soane's much-admired Pell Wall Hall, Shropshire, which burned down in the mid 1980s but is set to be rescued through the strenuous efforts of the local authority and a trust. The latest and in many ways saddest fire is that which consumed Uppark in Sussex in 1989. One of the great gems among country houses, as much for its now lost

S eaton House, Aberdeen which was destroyed by fire in 1963. Very few, if any, country houses were rebuilt after being destroyed by sometimes seemingly convenient flames. (Left)

C apenhurst Hall, Cheshire which has suffered a similar fate to Oulton Park, also in Cheshire, they have both been demolished.

contents as for its architecture, Uppark is – I understand – going to be rebuilt.

In the recent and less affluent past, many owners were forced to be hard and pragmatic. If there was no use for the old place and they couldn't afford the rates and upkeep, they got rid of it – and quickly. Many-turreted Panmure House and beautifully-sited Lindertis, both in Angus, were dynamited around 1955. So were several others at that time.

Other country houses were sold to developers and businessmen who saw a use for the estate, farms and other assets, but regarded the house as useless. Cheshire's Oulton Park, near Manchester, was bought and demolished in the 1920s. Today it is a racing car circuit. The same fate befell Leicestershire's Kirby Mallory House, demolished in 1953. Mallory Park racing circuit now lies in the grounds.

In their twilight years, some country houses changed hands many times as various people and organisations

sought to find a use for them. The delightful Maiden Erlegh in Berkshire was a classic example. Originally the seat of the Hyde family, it later passed through many hands, finally being bought around 1900 by Solly Joel, a South African gold and diamonds millionaire. After his death in 1931, the house successively became a boys' school, the headquarters for the Church Army and a camp for Hungarian refugees after the bloody uprising of 1956. Dilapidated and sad, it was demolished in 1960, the site cleared for new housing.

Boleyn Castle in Essex, also known as Green Street House, was no architectural jewel, being a picturesque warren of different styles spanning three centuries from 1550 to 1850. When it ceased to be used as a residence in 1880, it became a Catholic reformatory school (1889), a maternity home (1907) and was eventually leased to West Ham football club. It was finally demolished in 1955 and the entire site built over.

Whereas the destruction of huge houses with

hundreds of unusable rooms is at least understandable, the loss of small, but often exquisite, manors and mansions is particularly sad. Among the encyclopaedia of names here are Bradshaw Hall, near Bolton, demolished except for the porch in 1949–50 and the enchantingly named Sheepy Magna Hall in Leicestershire, a Georgian jewel demolished in 1956.

Other particularly sad losses are authentic Tudor, Elizabethan and early Jacobean houses, so few of which remain. Lancashire's Rawtenstall (demolished 1965) and the marvellous timber-and-whitewash Kenyon Peel Hall (demolished 1955) are two such, although another Lancashire beauty, Agecroft Hall, was taken down timber by timber and lovingly reassembled in Richmond, Virginia, in 1926.

Scrivelsby Court, Lincolnshire, once the home of the Dymokes, saw its ruined but redeemable remains flattened in 1956. Dorset's Tyneham Manor, for 250 years the seat of the Bond family and one of Britain's finest Elizabethan dwellings, was bought by the War office in 1939 for military training purposes which left it a derelict post-war shell finally demolished by the Ministry of Works in 1968.

If we lament the many houses which have sadly gone, we must also praise those organisations, ranging from the National Trust to the Landmark Trust to SAVE Britain's Heritage and countless others, without whose resolute commitment to saving our heritage and often dramatic interventions to save houses at risk the roll call of destruction would be many times worse.

It is also worth applauding the hundreds, indeed thousands, of individuals who have taken it upon themselves to buy, rescue and restore many country houses and other fine buildings which would otherwise have disappeared. A profile of some of these people and the tasks they have undertaken on make up the other half of this book.

Many country houses are still at risk. Some of Britain's many still-endangered houses are noted in the succeeding pages.

Dupplin Castle, Perthshire was the home of Lord and Lady Forteviot prior to joining the ranks of the demolished in 1967.

THE ROAD TO RESTORATION

LTHOUGH THERE WAS a sea change during the 1980s in public attitude towards Britain's endangered houses, with more and more people attracted to the idea of buying and restoring a big country house, there are still 100 to 200 notable houses at risk throughout the UK. Sadly, these may well stay in the 'at risk' or 'endangered' category for years or decades yet because of a number of factors.

The first is that, nearly all endangered country houses will cost much more to do up than they would fetch once fully restored. A house may be worth £500 000 or more fully restored, but if the restoration costs are £1.5 million, the restorer – even if the property is given to him – is going to lose £1 million on the deal.

In theory, grants from local authorites and other organisations, particularly English Heritage, should help make up the difference. But the experiences of many once-bitten, twice-shy restorers in obtaining grants in England are so discouraging that they cast severe doubt on the competence of the agencies providing these grants. A commendable exception to this rule seems to be CADW, (pronounced Cadoo) the equivalent of English Heritage under the Welsh Office, about whom I heard nothing but praise. It is also significant that some of the boldest and most interesting restorations I witnessed were in Wales.

The problem with obtaining grants is threefold. First, they take a long time to obtain; second, come with a lot of strings attached and, third, they are paid retrospectively based on submitted bills. Months, sometimes a year or more, may elapse between submitting bills and receiving the grant.

It is again significant that the 'professional' restorers – and those with the most experience – said they would avoid seeking grants, because of the delay and procrastination involved. The 'inexperienced' restorers – with one notable exception – confirmed the view of the professionals, but added that they were waiting for grant cheques and did not want to rock any boats until those cheques had come through.

On the question of grants coming with strings attached, the rules are generally that forty to fifty per cent grants will be allowed on the cost of key structural repairs needed to make the building solid, stable and watertight. The grants cover much structural work, but do not cover costs of water supply,

Glenmayne, Galashiels, is a miniature look-alike of Balmoral – with lush red interiors which emphasise the similarity.

plumbing, drainage, septic tanks, electricity, central heating, gas, decoration and many other things. These rate as 'comforts' and do not qualify for grant.

One can understand the bureaucratic reasoning behind that rule, but it can make things very difficult for a restorer keen to restore a house with a very ornate interior to something resembling its original condition, or where the costs of putting in acceptable plumbing, drainage, heating and electrical fittings can add up to more than half the total bill.

The advice to be distilled from all this is that the would-be first-time restorer should look for a small house which is a viable proposition without major grant aid. This should ensure that the restorer can complete the project without running up an insurmountable overdraft

and be able to clear his or her feet by selling the property once the work is finished. That does not mean grant aid should not be sought: it should, and if grants are offered and paid, that's encouraging. But the project should if possible be budgeted to break even or make a small profit without grant aid.

Should the restorer intend to stay in the house permanently after completion, he or she should try from the start to fund as much of the project as possible with a building society mortgage. In spite of the high mortgage rates of recent years, it is still the cheapest and least aggravating source of finance.

If a would-be restorer finds a much bigger potential project, he or she really needs to think long and hard about it. However strongly sentiment says – as it did to

David Pinnegar when he considered buying Hammerwood Park – this house must be rescued, the thought must be overridden with a rational question: what use and value will the house have once it is restored?

If the answer is 'something is bound to turn up', then forget it. The house will ruin the restorer as surely as the house has ruined itself. But if it appears that the house can be successfully divided up, by vertical or horizontal splitting, into several good-sized residences – for which there would be a market in the area – then it is seriously worth thinking about.

Suppose you – the potential restorer – have located, or seen advertised, a country house which, for all its decrepit, dilapidated or near-ruinous condition, strikes you as redeemable. What do you do next?

One of the great gems of Wales, Piercefield House in Gwent is crying out for restoration. It would, however, be an ambitious undertaking.

The answer is take an immense amount of advice. Weeks and months of it if necessary. Seek out, if you can obtain the information, the names of any other people who have looked seriously at the house recently or in the near past, ring them up and find out why they didn't buy it. Ring the local authority and winkle as much information as you can out of the planning department, building control, assessor and other people. Check with the local library for all background information on the house and even ask the local newspaper if they have a cuttings file on the house they will let you see.

If any one of the previous interested parties in the house tells you he had a structural survey done, see if you can obtain a copy from him or buy a duplicate from the structural engineer who did it. Alternatively, instruct an engineer or surveyor to do the job for you. It will cost you money, but a lot less than you could lose if you rush in without taking initial precautions.

If at this stage you have a clear idea of an end use for the restored house, and a basic feeling you can do the restoration within a budget that makes it a viable project, locate and put it to an architect as a proposition in principle, but not a full-blown commission as yet. Get him to draft basic drawings and a specification and ask a quantity surveyor to cost the quantities of materials and labour for the job. If you want a second opinion, ask several tradesmen – those you need, like bricklayers, masons, joiners, slaters and plasterers – to cost their sections of the project and put the list of materials to a building supplier, or several of them, for a quotation.

Once you get all the information back, sit down with your pocket calculator and add it all up, including interest, architect's fees and other professional costs. Be prepared for a shock. In ninety-nine cases out of a hundred, it will be much more than you reckoned.

The provisional work may well cost you four figures, by the time you pay the professionals and add up all the phone calls, car journeys, postage and rounds of drinks in pubs when you meet people. But it is still a bargain if you get reliable information that the restoration is not viable.

However, assuming the figures support your gut feeling that the project is viable, what do you do next? Talk at great length to your bank manager and see what sort of loans and backing you can get from him. Also go to your building society and see what they can offer. Add it all up and see what the gap is between what you've been promised and what you need. If it is a small gap, go back to the bank or building society and try and winkle enough out of them to close it. If it is a big gap, sit down and do some hard thinking.

Is it worth the hassle? Is it worth trying to get a grant? Are there ways of 'sweating' a few pounds out of the costs? Is there a way to do the restoration in stages which would allow you to sell a completed wing or section of the house early on in the project, bringing in extra money to finish the task?

If you opt to go ahead, then ask your solicitor to make a formal offer, subject to the title deeds being satisfactory. Once he has them, ask him to go over them with a fine tooth comb. Country houses and estates which have been sold off in bits and pieces are often a dog's breakfast for a solicitor, but he might spot some crucial flaws in the title which would make the house a very hazardous purchase. Alternatively, he might spot something which could be greatly to your advantage.

If after all this you still decide to go ahead, try to do as much as possible yourself. That does not mean trying to do the work of tradesmen – but, for instance, being your own clerk of works and getting everything organised. Order and pay for materials yourself, ensure they are delivered to site – or you go and collect them – so tradesmen are not sitting on site unoccupied because there are no materials for them to work with. Make sure you order things like skips and, if the house is such a ruin the men cannot shelter in it, buy an old caravan for them to be able to change and make tea in.

The cheapest way to get tradesmen is to employ so-called '714s' who pay their own tax and National Insurance and whom you pay a flat rate per hour or an agreed fee for the job regardless of hours. But try and

Before . . . the derelict face of the seventeenth-century mansion of Easter Elchies House, which overlooks the River Spey between Aberlour and Craigellaiche. After . . . the meticulous restoration of Easter Elchies House, which was carried out by Macallan-Glenlivet, who now utilise the attractive building as a visitors' centre.

agree that one senior tradesman is the accepted 'gaffer' with overall responsibility on site when you are not there.

Another important aspect is to work out your cashflow. That is not as hard as it seems, and is a very useful exercise. It is simply a question of working out when bills will fall due and ensuring the cash, from whatever sources, is there to cover them. You also have to keep a 'contingency fund' for unforeseen things – like the JCB accidentally digs up the water main and you have to

get a plumber in on the spot, or the gas bottle in the caravan runs out, or a trader offers you a load of old panelled doors at a knockdown price but they have to be paid for in cash.

Another important point about cashflow is do not get money too early. If work does not start until 1 March and payment on the first bills is not due until, say, late March or early April, it is foolish to draw a loan in early February on which you will have paid two months' interest before you've actually made use of it. Equally, make sure the money is there by the date bills are due, or you may have to make a lot of apologetic phone calls you would far rather avoid.

Another hint is that if you intend to sell the completely restored building, or restored parts of it, advertise it even before you have started work. If you get a buyer, or buyers, in advance, they can advise you about the kitchen and bathroom suites they would prefer and the colour schemes they want. Also, nothing helps you more than to have definite clients: they provide you with a very strong incentive to work to schedule and they help your standing at the bank, especially when they chip in with regular stage payments.

There is one final method for financing the restoration of a country house which, although I have not seen it applied to one, I have seen successfully used to restore a block of eight flats. It involves one person, maybe two, setting the idea in motion, and locating the right team. Essentially, eight people, or couples, or families – or as many groups of people as the country house can comfortably be split into homes for – set up a consortium. They buy the house, agree who gets which part of it and set out to restore it using their own professional and trade skills.

Ideally, one member of the team should be an architect, another a quantity surveyor, a third a structural engineer, a fourth an accountant, a fifth a lawyer. If the others are skilled tradesmen, the team is virtually complete. However, it is not essential that all members of the team fit the job descriptions above – but it helps because it greatly reduces the need to use outside, and that means paid, consultants or tradesmen. The more work that can be done by members of the consortium, the better. However, someone who is in transport or plant hire, or in the building supply trade or who is an excellent DIY decorator, can be just as valuable a team member in the long run.

At the outset, everyone buys a share in the consortium proportionate to the size and amenity of the dwelling he or she will eventually get and agrees to put in so much money and so many hours per month for the duration of the project. Those tasks which cannot be undertaken by members of the team will mean recruiting 714 labour for the duration of the project or casual labour for short bursts of activity when a lot of temporary manpower is needed.

By spreading the restoration costs among so many people and getting so much work done 'in house', means the restoration can be done for a fraction of the normal cost. It will still not be cheap, but it will be much cheaper than doing it any other way. The key is to find eight or more people prepared to join such a consortium and stick with it until the task is completed. It also means finding eight or more people who are attracted to restoring and living in the same country house.

One important point about the consortium. There needs to be very clear rules from the start, preferably drawn up by a lawyer and agreed by all the members, for the case of members who, either by decision or circumstance, leave the consortium before the house is complete. It must specify how they may sell their share to either another member or to a newcomer. This is to ensure the project keeps on the rails and to protect both those who stay in the consortium and those who may have to sell up having put a lot of money and hard work into the project.

Obviously, the consortium can decide all sorts of other matters and would possibly, once the project is complete, change itself into a management company to organise the running of the house and estate and to allocate repair and maintenance charges.

In spite of there being more interest than ever in restoration, there are many fine country houses still going to rack and ruin, some of them because they are too big for a single restorer and too isolated or costly for a big organisation such as Period Property Investment. A few enthusiastic and well-organised consortia might just fill that gap – and save some of Britain's still-endangered gems.

PART TWO

A CONTINUING
THREAT

NE LONG-FORGOTTEN historian once wrote that, in the ebb and flow of human endeavour, the ebbs and the flows eventually balanced themselves out. So we must reckon that the great tide of enthusiasm and vision which saw the British country house become one of the pinnacles of the civilised world – but which was subsequently destroyed by unstoppable changes in this nation's society – has now, quietly and unobtrusively, regained its former ascendancy. People of every social and financial background have come to realise the huge loss to our nation – and to the world – the destruction and obliteration of Britain's country house heritage has meant.

To the vast majority, this means quietly lamenting the losses while doing very little about it, other than paying a few pounds' subscription to the National Trust or other organisations and trusts dedicated to seeing our heritage kept intact. But to a visionary handful of people, this has meant investing their life savings, and much more besides, into the rescue and restoration of one particular house or castle which has caught their fancy.

The second half of this book is devoted to them and their ambitions. Some are (in the best sense of the word) gifted amateurs, some are hard-minded businessmen and women, some are great professionals who have devoted many years and hundreds of thousands of pounds to their chosen task. But all have one central and consuming vision – that a country house going to ruin demands its restoration to its former glory.... The glory that was home. The following pages follow the trials and tribulations of ten people who have set out on their self-chosen task.

The problem with any list of houses at risk in Britain is that it can change within a relatively short time-span. Houses which have stood neglected and derelict for decades can be bought for restoration when all hope for them had been given up. Equally, there are other houses regularly coming to the attention of SAVE Britain's Heritage and similar organisations and trusts.

All too often, houses only come to public attention when decay and dereliction are well advanced.

However, thanks to the efforts of historical and architectural groups and conservationists, the guardians of our heritage are probably given better advanced warning now of houses under threat than at any time before.

So, bearing in mind that this list, compiled at the start of 1990, may well change within a year or two, what follows is a summary of houses at risk in the century's last decade.

OULTON HALL, ROTHWELL YORKS

Built in 1822 around an existing small house by the noted architect Robert Smirke, rebuilt by his brother Sydney after a fire in 1850 and extended in 1870, this Georgian edifice lies just south of Leeds in parkland laid out by Sir Humphrey Repton. A mental hospital up to 1974, and prey to decay and vandalism since then, Oulton is currently on the market. Owners are Leeds City Council.

G*lentworth Hall, Lincolnshire built in 1753 by James Paine. It has lain empty for decades and narrowly avoided demolition in 1980. The current owner has restored the stables.*

GREAT BARR HALL, WALSALL, WEST MIDLANDS

This delightful small Gothic house, built 1777, and adjacent Gothic chapel, 1867, lie decayed and partly fire-gutted in the grounds of a mental hospital north of Birmingham. Its location is its downfall – being of no interest to private buyers and with neither the local council nor the health authority knowing what to do with it.

RUPERRA CASTLE, NEAR NEWPORT, GWENT

This four-towered castle, with battlements and high arched windows, was built in 1626 and improved after a fire in 1785. Used to station troops in the Second World War and hit by several fires since, the house is now a gutted shell with cows grazing in the once immaculate grounds.

EDWINSFORD HOUSE, NEAR LLANDEILO, DYFED

Another Welsh gem built in the seventeenth century, probably as two linked houses for two sections of the same family. Rambling, and with more than a touch of French chateau about it, it has been unoccupied since the Second World War and is rapidly decaying after lead was stripped from the roof.

GLENTWORTH HALL, LINCS

Built in 1753 for the 4th Earl of Scarborough by James Paine on the site of an older house, Glentworth consists of an incompleted main house and an extensive range of stables. Twelve bays wide and pedimented, the main house has been an empty shell for decades and narrowly avoided demolition in 1980. The current owner has restored a section of the stables as a residence.

YEATON PEVERY, SHREWSBURY, SHROPSHIRE

Another house high on every restorer's challenge list is this red sandstone Jacobean fantasy built as recently as 1890–92. Used as a girls' school until 1970 and unoccupied since, it is reported to be in surprisingly good condition for a building empty for twenty years. But is may well become a cause for deeper concern in the future.

HIMLEY HALL, DUDLEY, WEST MIDLANDS

A big house first built about 1720 and much enlarged in the 1820s, Himley has had mixed fortunes since the Dudley family moved out in the Second World War. First a hospital, then a regional headquarters for the National Coal Board, it was bought by the local council in 1967 and for twenty years housed Wolverhampton Polytechnic's School of Art and Design. Now empty but in relatively good condition, it would suit residential conversion.

PELL WALL HALL, MARKET DRAYTON, SHROPSHIRE

The last house built by the great Sir John Soane, this 1822 mansion has had a tragic history in recent years. A private residence until 1920, it was then used as a boarding school until 1962, and a corset factory until 1965. It was bought by a private buyer, leading to twenty years of neglect and decay. Repair notices from the local authority went unheeded and a compulsory purchase order was served in 1985. Protracted legal proceedings have ground on since then, with North Shropshire District Council acquiring the Hall in late 1988 to pass to the Historic Buildings Trust. Alas, a very mysterious fire in May 1986 reduced the Hall to a shell and the current estimate to restore it is 2.5 million.

LEDSTON HALL, CASTLEFORD, YORKS

A house with a long history, first built in the thirteenth century and with many additions and alterations since, Ledston hits the eye with its profusion of Jacobean 'Holburn gables' punctured by oval oculus windows. The long-fronted house has one wing and part of the main block occupied – split into five flats – but the rest of the building shows sign of severe decay. However, its layout would lend itself to a skilful horizontal or vertical split to form more private dwellings.

STOCKEN HALL, OAKHAM, LEICS

A fascinating, rambling house with Elizabethan, Jacobean and neo-Classical frontages, Stocken is a classic example of how to ruin a house by killing its setting and amenity. The grounds are used as a prison farm, a high mesh fence surrounds the house, various buildings have been built close by and a prison and a young offenders' institution have both been recently constructed, the former dominating the skyline. But there are hopes for Stocken as a craft centre and workshops.

EWART PARK, WOOLER, NORTHUMBERLAND

A strange but potentially delightful house built in 1787 and enlarged in 1867, Ewart's main frontage has a castellated Gothic wing and tower, a vernacular centre block and a Victorian extension wedged between high walls of what looks like a medieval keep. Empty and deserted, the house calls out for restoration before further decay sets in.

BUCKSHAW HALL, NEAR CHORLEY, LANCS

Another gem hemmed in by circumstance is this outstanding H-plan timber-frame house lying in the grounds of an armaments factory. Restored more than a century ago but empty since 1960, the house is a great cause for concern but would be of no interest to a private buyer because of its location.

There are several other Elizabethan and Jacobean houses in dire straits in the Lancashire and Greater Manchester areas. These include Stayley Hall at Stalybridge, Tameside, Stanley House at Mellor and Clegg Hall at Rochdale – though there are hopes Clegg Hall may be rescued by the Pennine Trust.

On the other side of the Pennines, Yorkshire also has a host of smaller houses in severe distress – including Hellaby Hall, near Maltby, Rotherham, Grimethorpe Hall at Barnsley, the severely dilapidated Paper Hall in Bradford, Swaithe House at Worsborough and Upper Shibden Hall, Halifax, which has an Italian-style campanile tower, unique in the area.

Humberside has a handful of neglected houses which are not so big as to be beyond the scope of a determined solo restorer. Names here include Swanland Hall, Swanland, and the Old Manor House at Elmswell, Driffield. But one house long on the danger list – Horkstow Hall, Barton-upon-Humber – is now being restored by a private buyer.

The growth of leisure and tourism has led to several long-empty country houses being finally bought and converted. Most notable name here is Llangoed Castle, Llyswen, Powys – one

A 1822 mansion, Pell Wall Hall has had a tragic history in recent years. A private residence until 1920, it was then used as a boarding school until 1962 and a corset factory until 1965.

*C*legg Hall, Rochdale which is currently abandoned but could be saved. (Right)

of a handful of stately homes built in the twentieth century – which has been made into a splendid hotel by the Laura Ashley organisation. Also destined to become hotels are Holme Lacy House, Hereford, Thoresby Hall, Leics, and possibly, Vale Royal Abbey, Cheshire. Plans are also afoot to convert long-neglected Woodfold Park, near Blackburn, Lancashire, into a golf course and night club.

However, conversion to housing units seems to be the most viable proposition at the moment, especially in the South and the Home Counties. Cams Hall, at Fareham, Hants, is being converted to dwellings, as have Ramridge House near Andover and Northwick Park, near Blockley, Gloucestershire.

But the biggest cheer of the late 1980s was heard when Revesby Abbey, near Horncastle, Lincolnshire – a magnificent Jacobean revival house built in 1843 – was compulsorily purchased from owners who had long neglected it. It is now being converted into individual flats and dwellings by a development group based at Wembley, Middlesex.

So we come to the final question.

*S*wanland Hall, Humberside – a Georgian Manor. (Below)

What hope is there for Britain's still-threatened country houses? The answer is in many ways an encouraging one. More than at any time this century, more people are aware of the problem and more people are keen to see those houses on the danger list rescued and restored. Also, there are more people with both money and a commitment to preservation prepared to take on the financial and organisational challenge of restoring a country house.

Having said that, there are still considerable problems affecting certain houses. There is still a handful of owners – both private individuals and local authorities – who for their own stubborn reasons will allow houses to decay and go to ruin rather than sell them to someone, or some organisation, who will restore them. There are still preservation organisations and societies who, for narrow purist reasons, will oppose and often kill off worthwhile restoration projects because they object to two per cent of the plan and cannot see the merit in the other ninety eight per cent.

There are still local authorities and local elected representatives who tend to view with suspicion anyone who sets out to restore a country house, assuming they are either rolling in money or are snobbish 'yuppies' the area could do without. The restorers I have met fall wholly outside both those categories.

Sadly, it would appear from what I have learned during my researches for this book that the main government channel in England to provide state grants to help private-initiative restoration projects is not doing a good job. It is said to be slow and unresponsive, particularly in matters of payment, which is counter-productive. At the time of writing, a new chief was appointed to the organisation and there is some hope that a 'new broom' may bring improvements. Unfortunately in this organisation of 1400 employees fewer than 200 are directly involved with the all-important field work. It is to be hoped with a change of management the running of the running of the organisation will be reviewed so that more people are out and about seeing what needs to be done and can thus speed the paperwork.

RESTORATION IN PROGRESS

HIGH HEAD, IVEGILL, CUMBRIA

Of the countless country houses which have passed from enduring splendour to near-total ruin in the years since the Second World War, two attract particular attention, one might almost say veneration, among architectural historians and other enthusiasts. They are at opposite ends of the country, but are similarly named – Highcliffe in Dorset and High Head in Cumbria.

The former is destined, the way things are, to go ever further to ruin, although there is hardly an architect or restoration specialist in Britain who has not at one time or another looked at it in the hope of finding the magic formula to rescue it from its plight.

High Head, on the other hand, has been relatively ignored – and as a result came perilously close to demolition on several occasions. However, High Head at long last is being rescued with 500 000 from English Heritage and more than 2 million from private financial sources. The man behind the rescue mission is Mr Christopher Terry, a Surrey-born but locally-resident architect and conservationist who – like so many people chronicled in this book – first became involved almost casually and finished up falling utterly under the spell of the house.

Once you see High Head, even as a gutted shell after the disastrous fires which consumed it in December 1956, you quickly understand why. It is a marvellous Georgian mansion of strong Palladian heritage in a setting which,

even after decades of utter neglect, is still beautiful and crying out to be restored.

It stands at the top of a hundred-foot densely wooded cliff above the River Ive – and indeed three quarters of a mile of fishing rights, twenty-six acres of woodland, terraced gardens and the Lord of the Manor title go with the building. The High Head woodlands lie on either side of the river and a Bailey bridge allows one to cross dryshod. These twenty-six acres are among the many remnants of the thousands of acres of forest which covered most of Cumbria for centuries. Indeed the original castle on the site – dating from 1270 or thereabouts – belonged to the de Harcla family whose tasks included guarding the forests and preventing poaching.

This was replaced, or added to, in Tudor times by a small but usable two-storey peel-tower, one wall of which still makes up most of High Head's unique western facade. This was in a pretty parlous state by the mid-eighteenth century, when the present building was started in 1744 by Henry Richmond Brougham. He was the dynamic, gifted scion of a long-established Cumbrian family who already had Brougham Hall at Penrith – which, by coincidence, Mr Terry is also retoring.

Henry Brougham (pronounced Broom) demolished a great deal of the Tudor structure at High Head and filled in the moat around it to create a garden. To enclose the Tudor remnant in the new edifice, a slightly prominent two-bay wing was built on to the west side of the main north facade, which gives High

Head its unusual asymmetrical appearance. The asymmetry was compounded in 1903 when a mundane low-rise two-storey cottage was built on to that wing to provide servants' accommodation.

In all, the main facade is thirteen-bay, whereas the rear – which can only be properly seen from fields a quarter of a mile across the Ive – is eight-bay with the most marvellous two-storey serliana or venetian window occupying the three bays in the centre of the facade. The short eastern facade has largely collapsed as a result of two earthquakes in 1979 and 1980. It has a beautiful neo-Classical two-storey pedimented entrance which cries out to be restored.

High Head is primarily of local brown-red sandstone ashlar, smoothly rusticated and with big quoins at all corners, with a lighter coloured sandstone used for pediments and decorative bas-relief Corinthian

Stocken Hall, Leicestershire presents a variety of facades from three architectural periods.

pilasters. It has a huge three-bay pediment at the centre of the main facade rising above the wall head line, with massive dentils and the Richmond coat of arms.

His son, Major John Waller Hills, who became an MP and Financial Secretary to the Treasury, inherited High Head in 1907. He in turn sold it in 1935 to Colonel Alan Gandar Dower, who became MP for Penrith and Cockermouth that year. Gandar Dower lost his seat in 1950 (he died in May 1980) and some time later sold High Head to the Robinsons, a family of butchers in Penrith. By 1954, the place was run-down, almost derelict. Fire destroyed it in 1956.

The shell, the still-habitable servants' quarters and the surrounding land were sold in 1959 to an ex-colonial official, Bill Dickman, for £800.

Mr Dickman tried on several occasions to obtain consent to demolish High Head and eventually received it in the early 1980s. However, the Department of the Environment under Michael Heseltine had the consent rescinded for two years, during which time a rescue plan for the house was to be organised. It was not and Mr Dickman re-applied after two years and actually had demolition men on site when Mr Terry intervened and bought High Head – in his own words – 'for the price of a good house'.

At the time of writing, the future of High Head looks more promising than at any other period since its great days at the dawn of this century. What adds to the current wave of optimism propelling Christopher Terry foward are the new prospects for Cumbria now oil has been discovered in and around the Solway Firth. If even a fraction of the inward investment which North Sea oil brought to Aberdeen and other east coast towns eventually comes to Cumbria, High Head – as a hotel or as a multi-tenancy residence – becomes a very interesting prospect indeed.

SINAI PARK, NEAR BURTON UPON TRENT, STAFFS

All the country houses I visited in the preparation of this book were in some way unique. But that term applied with special significance to Sinai Park. Unique by name, by location, by style, by the sheer totality of the restoration work being undertaken to bring it back to its former splendour. Indeed, former splendour may well be a slight misnomer, for Sinai Park was in its time not always meant to be the grand country house of a wealthy squire.

Although other houses I visited stood on sites where earlier houses had stood, Sinai Park is definitely the oldest one I saw still standing. More recent alterations and additions aside, it is also the most original. It stands on the site of an old Roman fort and is recorded in the Domesday Book. In the twelfth and thirteenth centuries it was a sanatorium either for monks, or run by monks, and indeed the name Sinai is believed to come from the French word *saignée* or *saigner*, which means 'bled' or 'to bleed', which was a common, if totally

ineffective, treatment in those days for many illnesses and conditions.

It is recorded that in 1247 the Abbot of Burton bought the house and it remained a monastic residence until the dissolution of the monasteries in 1547. It was then given, or acquired by, Sir William Paget, who rose to be Secretary of State, Lord Privy Seal and the personal ambassador of Henry VIII to France. It was to stay in the Paget family until 1911, with numerous alterations and modifications being made to it over the centuries.

About 1730 the moat was drained. During the eighteenth and nineteenth centuries, various brick-built additions were added, primarily on the west wing. Sinai Park's present owner and restorer, Mr Rodney Butcher, is going to great lengths to dismantle these so the house is restored as accurately as possible to its original Tudor timber shape and configuration.

Also some time in the latter part of the last century, Sinai Park's external walls were totally sheathed in an off-white harling, either to slow woodrot or to provide some form of weatherproofing, or because the Tudor bare-timber style was totally out of favour. An early aquatint postcard dating from the turn of the century shows the building as a mushroom-colour, but that may be due to the changing colour of the postcard rather than to the walls' colour in reality.

In 1911, the Pagets sold Sinai Park with some land to the local Co-operative as a working farm. About that time, the house was converted – either by the purchasers, or by a neighbouring farmer – into six farm labourers' cottages. From that time on, the fortunes of Sinai Park went steeply downhill. It changed hands three or four times, fell into ever greater disrepair, eventually became abandoned and derelict.

Local preservation societies, and national bodies such as SAVE Britain's Heritage and English Heritage, sought ways and means of rescuing Sinai Park – but the sad fact was the cost of rescuing it kept rising exponentially year by year. Yet it was such a rare and superb example of the Tudor manor house that the hope remained that someone would come along with the means, the expertise and the determination to undertake the task.

Of all the houses I visited, this conveyed the strongest impression of being rebuilt from the ground up. When it is complete, it will be one of very few totally 'new but original' timber-frame houses in Britain.

One can sense the majesty and magic of the house and I could well understand what had brought Rodney Butcher to it. It was the very fact it was in such desperate straits. There was so much to be done to rectify the neglect of decades, indeed generations. But Sinai Park had survived, and the fact it had survived was the challenge. If it had stood 500 years and more it deserved the right to stand for another 500. I certainly look forward to the day when I will see Sinai Park completed, which – according to Rodney Butcher – should be 1994.

CARNFIELD HALL, SOUTH NORMANTON, DERBYSHIRE

When it is complete, Carnfield Hall will be a quiet gem among country houses. What it may lack in grandeur and amenity, it will more than make up with its interior. Not just in its dark Elizabethan serenity and authenticity, but in the magic collection of antiques, bric-a-brac and collectors' marvels assembled over decades by Mr James Cartland who, with his wife Louise, bought Carnfield Hall as a near-ruin in 1987.

Delightfully, it is Mr Cartland's intention – more than that, his ambition – that the house and his amazing collection should eventually become an organic whole which people should come to see and appreciate. When that happens, a visit to Carnfield Hall will be a pilgrimage well worth making.

Carnfield lies on the outskirts of the Derbyshire village of South Normanton, on the south side of the main road to Alfreton, just three minutes drive from the M6. But those three minutes will take the visitor from the high-speed hassle of the late twentieth century to the quiet, dark-panelled peace of the sixteenth.

Although a house stood on the site before records were locally kept, the basic present edifice was started sometime during the fifteenth century. During the late sixteenth century, it was acquired by the Revell family and, in 1580, considerable alterations and extensions were made by Mr George Revell. His son, Edward, added to it in 1620 and built the great staircase which rises two floors from the main hall in the centre of the house. Further alterations were made in 1698 by another Revell, Robert, who is reported to have added a 'Georgian front'.

However, that may have been restricted to a semi-pediment above the front door and to replacing some of the old mullioned and transomed windows by timber-framed sash-weight ones. Otherwise, Carnfield remains very much a true Elizabethan manor house with some Jacobean overtones. Interestingly, there are still several original mullioned windows in the south facade which in many respects is as interesting as the main east frontage.

The house stayed the seat of the Revells until 1816, when the line died out. From then on Carnfield's lot was, in the words of the old song, not a happy one. It was put up for auction, failed to find a buyer – then was mysteriously bought by the man charged with auctioning it, Mr Joseph Wilson. About 1840, he was arrested on fraud and debt charges and died soon afterwards in Derby jail. However, the house stayed in his family until the death of his grandson, Vaughan Hobbs Radford, in 1912.

Then it was again bought by the man charged with the sale – Mr Melville Watson, an estate agent and surveyor. The house being in a run-down condition, he started on renovations. But not long into the work, he had an argument with one of his tenant farmers, who shot him dead in his office at Alfreton, then committed suicide.

Mr Watson's widow stayed in the house until her death in 1949, whereupon Carnfield Hall was sold to a Mr Derbyshire who owned an explosives factory only a few hundred yards away. Things went downhill and by 1959 the house was unoccupied. Mining subsidence under the north wing caused severe cracking in 1960 and the house was abandoned. In 1975 it was put up for sale and the plan was to demolish it and build a motel on the site. However, the plan fell through and Carnfield was bought by a Mr Webster who, whatever plans he may have had, further neglected the property. By the

Top, Carnfield Hall, showing the raised 'Georgian' parapet above the second-floor windows. Middle, the west frontage of Carnfield Hall looks on to a deep and pleasant garden. Above, the carved wooden hallstand at Carnfield Hall, is from Bernese Oberland.

*T*he east facade of Sheffield
Park (right) is like that of a
great abbey or cathedral of the
fourteenth or fifteenth century
with pointed arched windows.
(Top), the house tower at
Sheffield Park is straight neo-
Gothic, but this clock has an
Italian touch, especially to the
octagonal campanile-type top.
Wyatt at his most creative.

mid 1980s it was close to total collapse.

In 1987 it was bought by the Cartlands – who had been looking for some time for an original restorable period dwelling in which to store and eventually exhibit James Cartland's amazing collection.

The house is basically an H-shape Elizabethan manor with unusual twin gables on each 'foot' of the H but a high, straight wallhead line above the 'bar' of the H. The bar is three-bay with the main door replacing the middle ground-floor window. Above the door is an unusual broken pediment which runs into the sill of the first-floor window. Water from the main roof flows through four apertures in the high parapet and down four magnificent square-section lead downpipes.

The interior is a fascinating blend of its Elizabethan ancestry, coupled with later ideas and enhancements. There is, as always in an Elizabethan or Jacobean house, a large front hall with the large main staircase at the back opposite the front door. But the role of that hall seems to be more as a reception area or lobby, albeit a big one, rather than the traditional hearth of hospitality of earlier times. The room fulfilling that role is to be found on the floor above, just over the entrance hall and, with its dark wood panelling and ornate strapwork, is reckoned to be the best room of its kind in North Derbyshire.

Carnfield, on completion, will be a special gem well worth a detailed visit – particularly if James Cartland launches his proposed candlelit evening tours. The house has a certain aura of dark mystery about it – and it certainly has a lot of tales to tell. A combination of the house's great age, the amazing range of furniture, art, antiques and memorabilia which make up the Cartland collection and the heady blend of knowledge and enthusiasm which is a James Cartland hallmark, should make for a memorable visit.

SHEFFIELD PARK, SUSSEX

The Sheffield Park estate, originally spelled 'Sifelle', dates from pre-Norman times and passed through the hands of several families down the centuries. In 1769 it was sold – with a Tudor mansion and quadrangle on the present site – by the de la Warrs to John Baker Holroyd, who was elevated to the peerage eleven years later, first as Baron Sheffield and later as Earl of Sheffield.

In 1775 John Holroyd, as he then still was, asked the noted architect James Wyatt to produce plans to update the house. Wyatt's design is a classic piece of early 'Gothic'. This is the unique-to-Britain Gothic revival which started during the eighteenth century – largely as a reaction against the Italian classical and Palladian schools – and lasted until late in the Victorian era.

Sheffield Park was built quickly: it was virtually complete by 1778. Wyatt – nicknamed Wyatt the destroyer by his detractors for his propensity to part-demolish fine old churches and cathedrals and replace them with his own lesser creations – built some fine

houses, but he was noted for cutting corners to save money and time. Wyatt may have been on one restorer's mind when he commented to me – with a twinkle in his eye – 'Cowboy builders are by no means a twentieth century phenomenon'.

Sheffield Park was built quickly: it was virtually complete by 1778. Wyatt – nicknamed Wyatt the destroyer by his detractors for his propensity to part-demolish fine old churches and cathedrals and replace them with his own lesser creations – built some fine houses, but he was noted for cutting corners to save money and time. Wyatt may have been on one restorer's mind when he commented to me – with a twinkle in his eye – 'Cowboy builders are by no means a twentieth century phenomenon'.

While Sheffield Park was being built, the gardens were being landscaped by the two greatest names of the day – Lancelot 'Capability' Brown and Humphrey Repton. Their efforts produced gardens interspersed with lakes which are among the finest in England.

Wyatt's Sheffield Park is a very big

house and its restoration is a mammoth project; £5 million to be precise. It is not a task which one person could, or would, undertake on his or her own. It could only have been taken on by a 'commercial' restoration company which specialises in such work and has access to sources and quantities of finance such tasks require. Period Property Investment plc are in that league, having built up a good, and well-deserved, reputation for the work they do.

Based at St Albans, Herts, and run with great entrepreneurial skill by chartered surveyor John Nash and civil engineer Fred Eisenhart-Rothe, the firm takes on and restores near-derelict property which few other people would touch and brings it back to life. Much of their work over the past six years has been with derelict or run-down commercial property, but two of their country house successes have been Coln Manor, Wiltshire, and Ecton Hall, a 'Strawberry Hill Gothic' mansion just outside Northampton.

Sheffield Park is an unabashed 'enabling development' project. The vast main house is being split up into fifteen residences, ranging from modest two-bedroom flats to a huge five-bedroom, three-bathroom penthouse. In addition, there will be thirteen dwellings built around a large pedestrian courtyard close to the house. These dwellings will be two-storey, terraced and based on the old Victorian red-brick laundry which lies close to the former tradesmen's entrance. Finally, the two gate-lodges at the main entrance have been lavishly enlarged and extended. In all, there will be about thirty residences, not one of which will sell for less than six figures and many will be priced far higher than that.

John and Fred also give considerable thought to the future upkeep and viability of the houses they restore. In every instance they launch a house management company of which

all residents become members and pay annual ground rent and other charges to cover common external and internal maintenance, caretaker's wages and other costs. Both of them stay with the management company until it is running well

HAMMERWOOD PARK, NEAR EAST GRINSTEAD, SUSSEX

Less than twenty miles from Sheffield Park, another restoration project on another notable country house is nearing completion which is in every respect the antithesis of the enterprise at Sheffield Park. It is Hammerwood Park, which is one of only two houses in Britain designed and built by Benjamin Latrobe.

The restoration of Hammerwood Park is a real *tour de force* by one individual, David Pinnegar, who bought the house in a horrendous condition in June 1982. He had graduated in 1981 with a physics degree from Imperial College, London, and about that time inherited his late grandparents' house. He sold it and used the proceeds to buy Hammerwood. He also installed much of their period furniture in the house once it became habitable.

It was built in 1792 a few miles east of East Grinstead as a hunting lodge and country mansion to entertain friends and guests of Benjamin Latrobe's patron, John Sperling. It stood then in 3000 acres on a green and southward-sloping hillside close to Ashdown Forest which was then still abundant with game.

The house is classical without being Palladian – Latrobe was, along with Sir John Soane and others, an early rebel against strict Palladianism. At Hammerwood he has used features of Palladianism in interesting new ways.

There is no big central portico and pediment – but there are two delightful smaller porticos in the lower symmetrical wings flanking the main block.

There is a concession to the master in the four great pilasters which rise up to a prominent cornice between first and second floors. Indeed the second floor, above the cornice, looks almost like an afterthought, with the central three bays made slightly prominent to continue the external lines of the outer two pilasters. The main part of the house is five bays wide, each symmetrical wing four bays wide. All roofs are hipped and, unusually for the time, have no parapets or balustrades.

Hammerwood's special place in history has a transatlantic dimension. Born in Yorkshire in 1764 of French or Moravian parentage, Benjamin Latrobe was educated in France and Saxony, did the grand European tour, then studied architecture under S. P. Cockerell and engineering under Smeaton, the builder of the Eddystone Lighthouse. Hammerwood was Latrobe's first major commission, to be followed by Ashdown House two miles away, which is now a boys' school. Tragically,

*B*uilt on a south-facing slope looking towards Ashdown Forest near East Grinstead in Sussex, Hammerwood park is one of only two houses constructed in Britain by Benjamin Latrobe, who emigrated to America in 1792.

Latrobe's wife died in 1796 and, partly to flee his grief, he emigrated to the United States. He so impressed President Thomas Jefferson, no insignificant architect himself, that he became the first professional architect in the US – and certainly one of its greatest.

Hammerwood enjoyed an uneventful existence until the present century, being owned by the Sperlings, the Dorrien Magens, the Smiths of Smith's Bank and the Whidbornes – the family of a West Country clergyman – respectively. In 1919 it was used briefly to house thirty or more boarders of St Andrews School, Tunbridge Wells, after their school building burned down. Between the two world wars it was owned by the Pollen and Taylor families respectively.

As with many country houses, Hammerwood's problems started during the Second World War. It was requisitioned in 1939 or 1940 by the War Office to billet 200 soldiers. After the war, it was bought by the Chattell family, who obtained permission to convert it in to eleven flats. The conversion was far from ideal, the flats became unoccupied and in 1973 the house was sold to the pop group Led Zeppelin who intended to do it up as their rehearsal centre, residence and headquarters. Alas, their drummer died after an all-day drinking spree, their overseas commitments grew and their plans were shelved.

The house lay and rotted for nearly a decade. Thieves stole four tons of lead off the roof – and added insult to felony by rolling the lead across the roof slates, causing them to crack and break. Thieves also stripped the interior of anything of value and anything that was worth moving. By the time David Pinnegar saw it in the spring of 1982, it was an utter wreck, rated as a dangerous structure and had water pouring in through fourteen separate gaps in the roof. Wet and dry rot were rampant and fruiting bodies – ghastly bloated brown

fungi normally seen on dead or dying trees – grew malevolently from the rotting walls. The floors were thick with a sticky brown dust – the spores – and most of the upstairs rooms had giant skylights where the ceilings should have been.

Eventually, after being told the house might well collapse if left in its current state for another winter, he swallowed hard and bought it in June 1982 – and promptly vowed he would have it sufficiently restored to open at least part of it to the public the following Easter; that duly happened.

The work is not yet complete. Indeed two rooms have been left with the floor and ceiling between them collapsed (though with the fallen timbers and plaster removed) to show visitors the state the house was in when first bought. That will shortly be rectified. But otherwise much of the work has been done.

Were Benjamin Latrobe alive today, he would be delighted to see his Sussex creation in such uniquely capable hands.

GUNTON HALL, NORFOLK

Among the great country house doctors of our time one name stands supreme – Kit Martin.

His approach has worked very successfully at Gunton Hall, a great rambling, fire-gutted Palladian-Georgian pile in deepest Norfolk which he has transformed into a splendid living community and where he and his wife, Sally, live. They first saw Gunton in 1979, about the time the last of the Harbords, who had owned Gunton for centuries, died. He wrote a letter to the agents asking for an option on the property if it ever came up for sale. A reply came by return of post and the Martins bought it.

Gunton is a fascinating house. Originally an Elizabethan mansion

stood on the site, but few vestiges of it can be found anywhere. A two-storey Palladian house facing south was started in 1742, designed by Matthew Brettingham – who was building nearby Holkham Hall – for Sir William Harbord. After his death in 1770, his son, the first Lord Suffield, commissioned both Adam and Wyatt to plan a major addition to the house, with an entire new frontage facing east.

Between 1778 and 1785, these great additions were built in a line northward from the existing Palladian house. These were not just a main residence, but also servants' quarters, game larder, brewery, stores and stables. Wyatt's original plans showed the stables as a huge enclave around a circular courtyard: in fact, more modest stables around a square courtyard were built. An Adam suggestion – to build two symmetrical conservatories flanking the orginal Palladian front and linked by a deep colonnade – was finally carried out in the 1820s, and very effective it is too.

Gunton in the nineteenth century was a very grand place indeed, with hundreds of acres of fine parkland landscaped by Gilpin, two lakes and an amazing 100-foot tower dominating the north entrance of the estate. It is unsurprising, therefore, that the Prince of Wales, later Edward VII, liked Gunton so much he and his retinue became regular visitors. It is rumoured that the Harbord family, unable to shoulder the cost of these princely visits, set fire to the Palladian section of the house so they had a cast-iron reason for cancelling future invitations. That fire in 1872 marked the start of Gunton's decline and fall, and a century later the last two surviving Harbords were down to living in a section of one wing of the once magnificent but, by then, wholly decayed house.

Kit Martin's restoration is both ingenious and delightful. Every edifice in the Gunton complex has been restored and put to use as a private

An attractive corner of Gunton Hall which has been restored as a series of private residences. It is a marvel of Palladian architecture built in 1742 by Matthew Brettingham.

dwelling. The work was done in phases and, as each group of dwellings was completed and sold, the money was ploughed back into the next phase of the enterprise.

One feels that Kit Martin is quietly pleased with the outcome of the long programme at Gunton, although he never says so in so many words. But Gunton struck me as a very successful formula for achieving what might initially have seemed a hopeless task. And residents I spoke to casually while strolling in the grounds have high praise for the house, the setting and the balance which has been struck between privacy and community. If there were such a thing as an approval rating for country-house restoration projects, Gunton must rate in the high nineties. Much if not all of the kudos for that must go to Kit Martin.

PLAS TEG, NEAR MOLD, NORTH WALES

There is a cluster of restorations in North Wales, two of which are being undertaken by the same restorer – Cornelia Bayley. With an infectious energy and enthusiasm, Cornelia is a former antiques dealer and businesswoman endowed with great determination. She certainly needs it. The restoration of one country house can be a killer of a task: to undertake two – though admittedly one was virtually complete before serious work started on the second – is an Augean enterprise.

The two Augean stables Cornelia has set out to restore are Plas Teg, near Mold, and nearby Bettisfield, near Hanmer, lying in a little pocket of Wales enclosed on three sides by Shropshire. Cornelia makes no bones about the fact that she fell in love with Plas Teg from the moment she saw it advertised in *Country Life* in the late spring of 1986.

Travelling from Lincolnshire, where she then lived, she looked it over and promptly instructed her solicitor to offer for it. The eventual agreed price was £75 000.

The house might not have been everybody's taste either. Built by Sir John Trevor in 1610, it is a high-fronted H-plan house with bold square towers at all four corners, topped by ornate turrets which look as if they should have bells in them but only one does. Four high chimneys stand at each corner of each tower (an intriguing solution to the problem of the great banks of chimneys which clutter the roof-lines of many other houses) and the front facade is further enhanced by three very ornate Jacobean pediments. The windows are an unusual mixture: some have wooden mullions and transoms, others appear to be sash-weight with astragals, but are in fact fixed with small opening casements.

The massive oak and wrought iron front door stands in a short projecting porch with Jacobean pediment flanked by two single windows. The house is five-bay along the main facade, which looks roughly north-eastward across rolling countryside towards the Mersey. A dual-carriageway main road runs only fifty or sixty yards away, but because the road line is sunk well beneath the landscape line, one is unaware of it.

The interiors date mostly from the time of William VI, but struck me as very Jacobean, even Elizabethan. Dark wood panelling is very much in evidence, especially on the great main staircase which climbs from ground to first floor at the eastern end of the house. There is a much simpler servants' stairwell at the western end. There is a great main hall on the ground floor reached directly through the front porch, with a similar if smaller room above it on the first floor. The grand staircase does not proceed beyond the first floor: a much smaller staircase in the eastern rear tower leads on the upper floor.

Guests cannot complain they are staying in a house devoid of interest. In its history, Plas Teg has seen some turbulent moments and witnessed more than its share of human tragedy. Not without reason it is thought to be one of the most haunted houses in Britain.

It is said that around the year 1600, about 10 years before the present house was built – but when an earlier house doubtless stood on the same site – Sir John Trevor's teenage daughter, Dorothy, met a terrible death. Forced to become engaged to a man chosen by her parents, she planned to elope with her true love, a local boy called Iorwerth. The couple agreed to use a well near the house as a rendezvous. However, in advance of the agreed night, the young woman hid her jewels beside the well.

On the appointed night, she went out to uncover her jewels and was unable to find them. Digging with her bare hands, she lost her balance, fell in to the well and drowned. Her family, finding her gone and her jewels missing,

Plas Teg seen from the east. Note the towers with the 'belfries' above – only one has a bell – and the ingenious location of the chimneys at each corner. (Above)

A four-poster bed with ornate period drapes should aid profound slumber in Plas Teg, reputedly one of Britain's most haunted houses.

A supreme staircase at Plas Teg – the east staircase with its ornate, intricately carved newel posts forms part of the house's splendid interiors.

immediately suspected Iorwerth. He admitted that they had been planning to elope but said he had turned up at the agreed spot only to wait three hours before returning dejectedly home.

Months later, Dorothy's body was found in the well, but there is no mention of the jewels ever being found. Iorwerth, either driven to despair by her disappearance or unable to face constant suspicion, hanged himself.

A not dissimilar legend, set about 200 years later, tells of a beautiful daughter of the house who was pursued by two suitors. When out riding with her favourite, they ran into his rival. A duel erupted, her favourite was killed on the spot and the distraught girl galloped frantically back to Plas Teg followed by the victor. Rather than submit to him,

she gathered her jewels from her room and flung them and herself into the well where she drowned.

All in all, Plas Teg is a house whose history would justify a book of its own. In brief, it stayed in the Trevor or Trevor Roper families, through periods of great joy and great tragedy, until the First World War. The last-but-one owner with family links was Capt. Charles Cadwaladr Trevor-Roper, who was killed in August 1917. His widow remarried and moved to London.

Tenanted in the inter-war years, Plas Teg was used to billet US Servicemen in 1944, and was then sold to local auctioneers who used it as a furniture store. From 1947, it was used briefly by the NAAFI, but they moved out and the house fell into disrepair. In 1958 it was extensively repaired by Mr Patrick Trevor Roper and for 20 years it had a succession of tenants. It was bought in 1977 in a rundown state by a couple who were unable to maintain the house adequately. Finally, with the house in direst straits, the house was bought in 1985 by Cornelia Bayley

TREVOR HALL, RUABON, LLANGOLLEN, CLWYD

When Trevor Hall is fully restored, it will – I am sure – hold a special affection in the memories of everyone who visits it. Not just because this country house lies in such a charming position looking south across the valley of the river Afon near Llangollen, but because of the friendliness and hospitality of its restorer, Michael Tree. All the restorers I met had personality and charm, but Michael had both in abundance, coupled with a deep-seated single-mindedness about the house he is bringing back to glory from near-oblivion. Such single-mindedness is needed: he faces as awesome a task as

any I saw.

Trevor Hall is an interesting mixture. The building was probably constructed in the mid-sixteenth century, but about 1740 it had new Georgian main (south) and eastern facades added. The main facade is in red brick, with pale stone quoins, sills, window keystones and string courses, but the west facade and much of the rear is still in the original stone and rubble. The windows in the south and east facades are sashweight with thin astragals, whereas those on the west facade are much older with wooden mullions and leaded lights. These factors, plus the ground floor layout, lead one to conclude the house had an earlier, possibly Elizabethan or Tudor, south facade, demolished to make way for the current one.

One book describes Trevor Hall as Baroque, but it would not appear so to me. The house is too simple, austere even, to be described as Baroque – and the building's only pediment (above the substantial but hardly grandiose front door) is complete, not the broken pediment which is the hallmark of much Baroque design.

The roof of Trevor Hall is also a cause of design debate. The orginal 1740s house is thought to have had a plain, hipped grey-slated roof, but after a severe fire in the early 1960s, a cheaper flat roof was installed. At some point, too, a hefty red brick parapet was built along the south facade. It adds to the sense of height and grandeur of the frontage, but the bricks are different from those of the rest of the facade and the parapet's weight is visibly adding strain to the main frontage structure.

Michael Tree intends eventually to remove the parapet and re-install a full hipped roof, and so restore Trevor Hall to its original 1740s appearance. But, showing a touch of genius, he intends to lower and retain the present flat roof to provide a floored attic under the new roof. Definitely a case of making good use of what is there and a virtue out of necessity.

The house is a shallow H-plan, with the main entrance door in the traditional position, at the centre of the bar of the H, leading to a big but not huge main hall with the main staircase, dark oak with ornate balustrades and newel posts, leading off to the left. This again leads one to suppose Trevor Hall is basically an older structure with a 1740s frontage and other improvements.

Several of these 'improvements', including massive kitchens built during the Victorian era at the rear of the house, were totally out of keeping with the rest of the structure and have been demolished. Although the rear facade of Trevor Hall is very much the poor relation to the front one, it now displays a good measure of design and architectural coherence which it certainly would have lacked with all the Victorian appendages and outhouses.

Trevor Hall belonged for centuries to the Trevors, descended from the Earls of Hereford and married into the Welsh Prince's family. About 1820, however, the big family estates were divided and the family moved to Coed-Helen near Caernarvon. It stood empty for years, and was then leased to the manager of a local foundry, a Liverpool shipping magnate and eventually – on a long lease – to a successful brick manufacturer Mr J.C.Edwards, who put on the extra parapet with his own bricks.

The house stayed with the Edwards as tenants for nearly a century until J.C.'s son Lloyd, then in his nineties, moved out to stay with his daughter in 1952. The house stood empty for several years, then was sold in 1960 to a timber merchant, who tried to obtain demolition consent but failed because of objections by the local villagers. It was then sold to the WRVS whose efforts to convert it to a hostel were ruined by a bad fire in 1964. It then stood roofless for three years, was bought by a neighbouring farmer who simply re-roofed it as a store and livestock shelter. Michael Tree first saw it in 1979 and spent eight years negotiating the purchase of it and enough land from the farmer. It finally became his in 1987.

Hence, the green slopes in front of Trevor Hall are pasture and farmland and will doubtless stay so in perpetuity. However, the approach to the hall, along a straight drive lightly inclined through a plantation of dark conifers, has presented Michael Tree with a problem not unlike those faced by some other restorers.

Michael's enthusiasm and affection for Trevor Hall are infectious. As he and others said to me, the house takes you over.

In Trevor Hall, he has a couple of rooms, all bare floorboards, thin partitions and blank stone walls, where he keeps check on all the work in progress and the bills. He is not without company: although many of the tradesmen are from local villages, the main builder, Dennis Wright, who comes from the Home Counties and has many successful restoration projects to his credit, lives permanently in Trevor Hall and plans to do so for the duration of the task, which may take four years.

Although Michael is no builder himself, he contributes to the overall task, largely by tracking down suitable building materials – timbers, doors, fireplaces, panelling, plasterwork and 101 other items – locally and further afield. He scans the papers for news items and advertisements and has sought help from local libraries and archivists for information on the house, its earlier appearance and its contents. His sleuthing work occasionally pays handsome dividends. He was able to obtain five or six magnificent Victorian cast-iron baths, plus plumbing, for 65 to a charity, which was being thrown out during a modernisation project.

His post at the Crown Estates helps, too. He is able to seek advice and help from a very wide range of people with whom his work brings him into contact. But it would be wrong to suggest or imply that Michael has advantages which other restorers do not; quite the contrary. He is doing things the hard way, has sunk his life savings and has committed much of his monthly salary for years on end to the restoration of Trevor Hall.

Michael's greatest quality is his enthuasiasm. The day I was there he was host to a twenty-five-strong group of visitors from the Georgian Society and completed a fascinating tour with a marvellous afternoon tea served buffet-style in the main hall from which as many building materials as possible had temporarily been removed. If he can produce such hospitality and style in what is still largely a building site, it is worth waiting to see with what marvels he will delight guests once Trevor Hall is complete.

Trevor Hall – an interesting mixture it was probably constructed in the mid-sixteenth century, but in about 1740 it had new Georgian main (south) and eastern facades added.

Top, Buntingsdale Hall built in 1721 based on drawings of Francis Smith, Warwick. Above, the big red-brick Georgian mansion with matching extension built in 1857.

BUNTINGSDALE HALL, MARKETDRAYTON, SHROPSHIRE

Market Drayton is a small, pleasant Shropshire town not far from Stoke-on-Trent, which could be a very passable real-life version of Borchester in the BBC radio series, 'The Archers'. It is also the location of two of Britain's most notable country houses at risk – Pell Wall Hall and Buntingsdale Hall.

The former is, alas, a gutted shell after a disastrous fire in 1986, but at the time of writing Herculean efforts are being made by the local district council and many conservationists to rescue it. Buntingsdale Hall, on the other hand, is already well down the road to redemption thanks to a bold initiative by the Mackworth family.

The Mackworths, Richard and Rosalind, and their two daughters, Julia and Victoria, are descendants of one of the notable families who had Buntingsdale as their country seat in earlier times. On hearing of the house's endangered status, they set out to rescue it – as much from the legal red tape in

which it had become ensnared as from the dangers of dry rot and vandalism that threaten all abandoned country houses. Although they still have a long way to go, the Mackworths have already achieved a great deal. Like Michael Tree does at Trevor Hall, they stay in London during the week, but spend many if not most weekends hard at work at Buntingsdale.

The original house was built in 1721, based on designs by Mr Francis Smith, Warwick. It is red-brick Georgian with four pilasters rising to the top of the first floor where there is a substantial projecting cornice. Above that lies a lower-ceilinged and smaller-windowed second floor topped by a balustrade and neat central pediment with an oval motif in the tympanum.

Unusually, the house has virtually identical east and west-facing facades, and a beautiful, bow-fronted south-facing facade. The main facades of the original house are nine bays wide, with slightly-arched sash-weight windows with slim astragals. However, the top-floor windows are rectangualar.

In the 1850s, a substantial extension was built to the north and, later again, an annexe beyond. Although the north extension has one storey fewer than the main house, it has been built with great regard for the original structure – which is unusual for Victorian extensions: all too often the extension would be in Gothic or another style, totally altering the house's appearance and character.

At Buntingsdale, only slight differences at the heads of the pilasters and slimmer chimneys reveal that this section is 130 years younger than the original house. The effect of the extension is to break the original, almost Palladian symmetry of the original edifice, but it is certainly very pleasant to look at and in no way detracts from Buntingsdale's impressive aura. Indeed, a careful effort has been made to restore an element of symmetry by building an extra room on the second floor at the

northern end, almost a flattish tower, to provide continuity with the roof-line of the main structure.

Buntingsdale is a big house, fourteen bays wide, three storeys high plus basement for much of the area it covers. It stands in substantial grounds at the end of a short but imposing tarmac approach road leading to a roundabout in front of the main door.

Buntingsdale's troubles started when the RAF moved out in 1981 and it was sold to developers called Readygrange. They set out to convert it – by a vertical split – into individual residences, five in the main building, one or more in the annexe. They obtained planning permission from the local authority, even though their plans involved a breeze-block access stairway to a first-floor window and a crass modern staircase leading straight out of the dining-room, destroying some fine plaster ceiling work in the process.

However, very little was done before the company ceased trading. In that time, however, all parts of the building had been sold to buyers who in turn had obtained mortgages, mainly from building societies, to finance initial purchase and, presumably, the costs of modernisation and decoration. With the demise of Readygrange, the whole project slid into quicksands and the building started to deteriorate rapidly, especially after four tons of lead were stripped from the roof.

Buntingsdale looked set to join the great herd of stately white elephants in the slow graveyard of decay when the Mackworths appeared on the scene. The grandson of a previous owner, Richard Mackworth and his wife bought one section of the house from the Abbey National Building Society and have since acquired a second section. They hope, by dogged legal sleuthing and sheer perseverance, to be able to buy the entire building and perform a complete restoration.

TILLYCAIRN CASTLE, NEAR ALFORD, ABERDEENSHIRE

If much of England has seen a severe cull of its many country houses, Scotland, like all of Britain's Celtic fringe, has witnessed wholesale slaughter. With just one tenth of the UK population, Scotland has seen the destruction of 400 country houses in the past century, or twenty per cent of the UK total. The tally for even-smaller and less-populated Wales is about the same, but the houses demolished in Scotland were in general bigger and more magnificent. This is because many if not all of those demolished were built in the Victorian era by the top ranks of commerce as hunting and shooting lodges, or summer homes, rather than as family seats for the aristocracy or landed gentry.

Not that there weren't some truly amazing family seats built. Hamilton Palace in Lanarkshire, abandoned because of mining subsidence in 1892 and demolished in 1922, was regarded as one of the greatest country houses in the world in its day. The residence of the Dukes of Hamilton, it was so grand that even the palace kennels, now restored as part of Chatelherault Country Park near Motherwell, are regarded as architectural masterpieces. Or again, no one would sniff at the phantasmagorical Dunrobin Castle, the seat of the Dukes of Sutherland, all turrets and 400-plus rooms overlooking the Moray Firth north of Golspie.

As in England, the wholesale destruction of Scottish country houses has at long last stopped – but for slightly different reasons than south of the border. One short-term reason has been the early introduction of community charge to replace rates.

However, for the enthusiastic restorer, Scotland is awash with thousands of abandoned castles, towers and keeps, ranging from the remarkably intact to those now little more than a pile of stones in a cow pasture, crying out to be lovingly rebuilt. One such pile of stones less than a decade ago was Tillycairn Castle, midway between Alford and Kintore, about thirty miles west-north-west of Aberdeen. Even as a ruin it still stood nearly its full height, but all of the roof and great piles of masonry had caved in to the centre of the edifice; all timber had long since rotted away or been used as firewood and trees and bushes grew from nooks and crannies in the decaying stonework. But for a building which had lain abandoned since 1720 or 1722, it was still 'all there' – which also says something about the strength and workmanship of the original masonry.

In 1972, it was bought by David Lumsden, a conservationist and amateur genealogist, who had returned to the UK in 1969 after many years' service in India and Africa. On his return, he set out to restore Old Cushnie House, an Aberdeenshire mansion with which he had strong family connections, at a time when such restoration projects, especially in Scotland, were relatively if not totally, unheard of.

He did not actually start work on Tillycairn until 1980 – he sold Old Cushnie House in 1979 – and was regarded as utterly mad by many friends and colleagues for taking on so daunting a project. But David was far from mad – just well ahead of his time. He was told it would take at least five years: he completed the task in under eighteen months, and for probably half the money it would have cost had he put the task out to a contractor. His secret – echoed by so many other successful restorers – is 'If you're prepared to do it yourself, do it yourself!'

That does not mean mixing every barrowload of cement or lugging all the heavy timbers single-handed. It means finding the best and most cost-effective method for doing the job. As we sipped whisky in the main hall of Tillycairn under a mural above the fireplace copied from ancestor Matthew Lumsden's paintings at Provost Skene's house in Aberdeen, David spelled out his formula for efficient, effective restoration.

The key, he declared, is getting an excellent clerk of works who does all the organising and logistics, the ordering and progress chasing, and who acts as your site agent and right-hand man for the duration of the work. To draw an analogy from industry, the clerk of works is the general manager who keeps the day-to-day work flowing while you are the chairman, taking the final decisions and paying the bills.

David Lumsden's clerk of works was Ian Cumming, who has since gone on to oversee several notable restoration projects, the most recent being Forter Castle, Glen Isla, Tayside. With him and a very small labour force – a mason, a stonecutter, two labourers and a plasterer, plus joiners as and when they were needed – the whole task was completed in a quarter of the time and at half the cost many had predicted.

Not that there wasn't a great deal to do. Great quantities of collapsed masonry had to be painstakingly removed and placed outside, vegetation uprooted from nooks and crannies where it grew without triggering the collapse of more stonework.

The entire project was done without modern materials such as bricks or breeze blocks. Original rubble and stone – some of it lying scattered around adjacent fields – was used in the reconstruction, held together by 135 tons of mortar carefully mixed on site. Plans for the work were drawn up on the basis of old drawings and sketches of the building, and on careful observation of the ruin itself – for instance, looking for gaps in the masonry for floor joists and other long-vanished timbers.

*L*ess than a decade ago Tillycairn Castle was little more than a pile of stones, its restoration was achieved using no modern materials.

ARCHITECTURAL STYLES

One of the elements which has been an essential part of the history of the country house is the development of architectural styles. This development can be illustrated by specific features that show in detail the changes which occurred over the centuries.

DOORWAYS, PORCHES AND PORTICOES

1 An early Tudor hall 'screens' oak doorways, later panelled versions were made in the linenfold design.

2 An ornate doorway of the early sixteenth century. Very few domestic doorways which predate the fifteenth century exist.

3 An example of Elizabethan style, the orders which flanked doorways often consisted of carved figures, grotesques, flowers, fruit and animals.

4 The design of Jacobean doorways developed from the Elizabethan to encompass strapwork decoration on the plinths beneath the columns or pilasters.

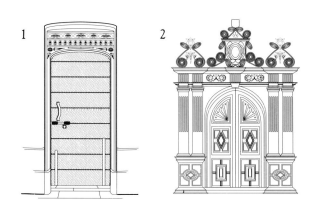

WINDOWS

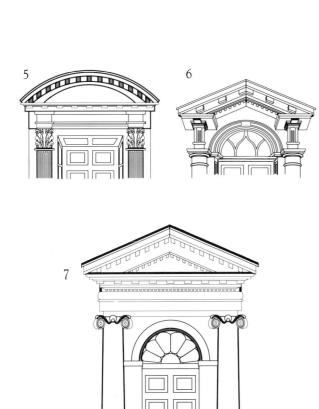

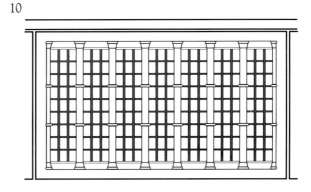

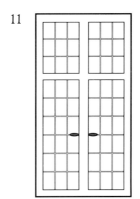

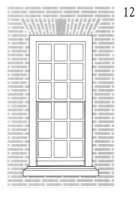

5 An early Georgian doorcase with a curved pediment – a style based on the Corinthian classical order.

6 Another early Georgian example, with a design based on the Ionic order of classical architecture. The use of semi-circular fanlights was by now a popular feature.

7 A Gothic-influenced fanlight surrounded by a broken entablature and triangular pediment make up this mid-Georgian design.

8 Another classical influence – this time from the Greek Doric order, illustrated by an example of a late Regency portico.

9 A sixteenth century oriel window, during this century windows became much larger as glass was more commonly used to make up larger casements from small rectangular or diamond panes.

10 In the Elizabethan period tracery gradually disappeared from window designs and rectangular frames were a common feature.

11 Although this is an illustration of a typical pre-Georgian mullioned and transomed double light the overall proportions are very similar to later sash windows.

12 A classical early Georgian window with thick glazing bars and the frame only just set back from the face of the wall.

13 A late Georgian Gothic casement window – there is a drip mould above helping to protect the pointed tracery work.

14 An eighteenth century Adam design. A classical style typical of the rectangular form of the period, pedimental or horizontal head mouldings were also a frequent feature.

15 An earlier eighteenth century window by Vanbrugh. Many designs were put together in two or three lights with balustraded parapets beneath.

16 A Georgian window opening framed by stone architraves, frieze and pediment with consoles.

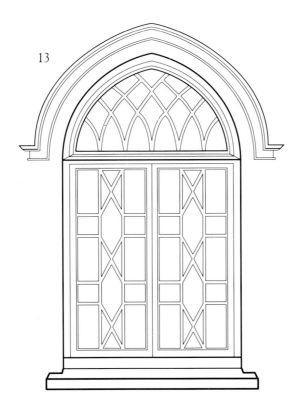

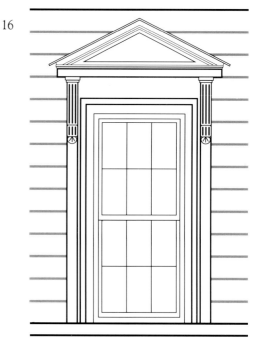

STAIRCASES

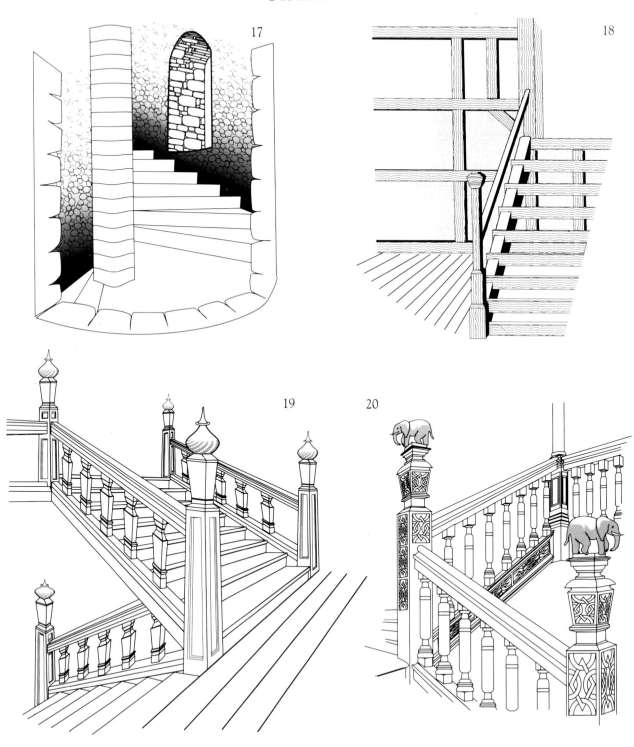

17

18

19

20

17 An early Medieval stone newel staircase, the whole spiral was normally constructed in a turret or tower.
18 A fourteenth century ladder design, typically made of wood, this type were well constructed, although primitive, and often used as a means of reaching a solar or bedroom from the main hall.
19 An Elizabethan carved oak 'dog-legged' staircase – so called because it was built in short flights of six to ten stairs with each flight turning back alongside the one immediately above and below it.
20 A Jacobean carved oak staircase – by this period the staircase had evolved into a magnificent feature. It was usually constructed around an open well taking up much more space and had decoratively carved newel posts at the top and bottom of each flight, surmounted by carved finials.

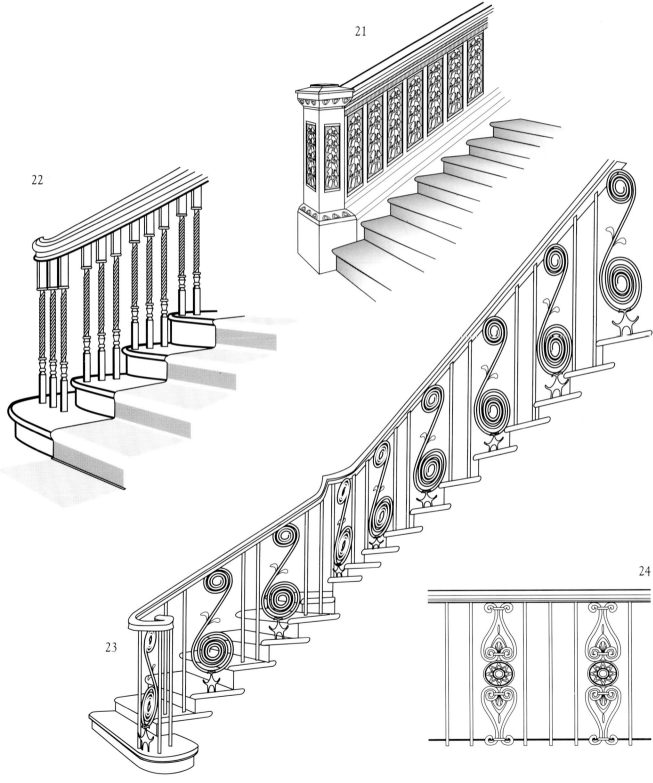

21 A carved wood panel balustrade design of the mid-seventeenth century. Individual balusters had been replaced by a continuous carved and pierced panel, while newel posts had become less ostentatious.

22 A typical example from the first half of the eighteenth century, this staircase would have had polished mahogany treads and delicate balustrades either of the barley-sugar design or turned vase shapes.

23 A mahogany banister rail, marble stairs and wrought-iron scroll balustrade indicative of the second half of the eighteenth century.

24 An early Victorian balustrade and handrail, these designs were often cast, rather than wrought-iron and were coarser than their Regency predecessors.

FIREPLACES

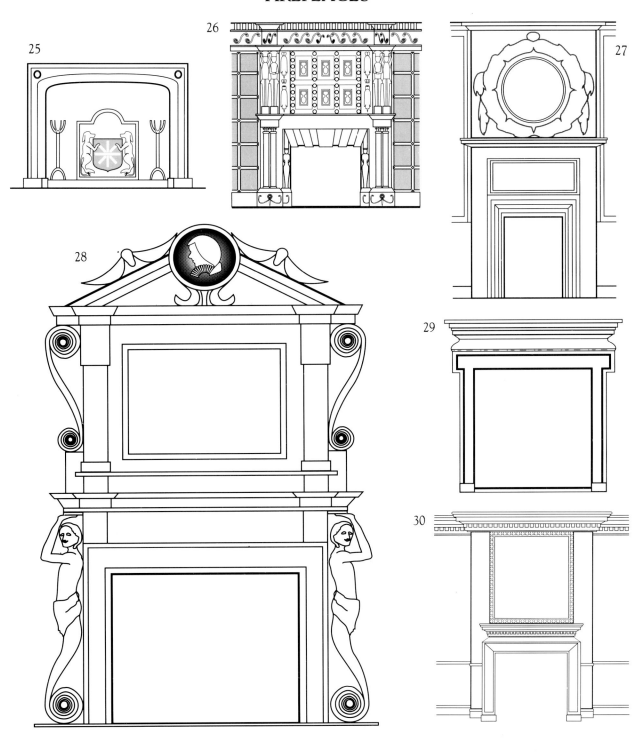

25 An example from the Tudor period. The Tudor arch was gradually replaced by a rectangular opening with ornamental decorations.

26 A later Tudor fireplace, designs had begun to change dramatically as imported artists introduced the first features of the Renaissance.

27 During the seventeenth century classical designs using marble, stone and plaster became popular. This design is in the style of Inigo Jones and represents a marble mantel shelf of full height.

28 Another seventeenth century example, the over-mantel mirror and china shelves. The position in the plan of the fireplace had now become subordinate to the importance of symmetry.

29 Much favoured during the Georgian period the Queen Anne fireplace with narrow shouldered architrave was redeveloped by Robert Adam.

30 An early Georgian fireplace with entablature above, showing the bolection moulding typical of this period.

31 Fireplaces with plain mouldings were replaced by those with a shouldered architrave and inverted scrolls at the side. A keystone or tablet above the opening to break up the line of the entablature was another innovation.

32 & 33 Adam style mid-Georgian fireplaces fitted with grates. A familiar element of the surround is the central plaque on the frieze.

34 A medieval stack crowned with an iron cap giving a decorative feature which was also intended to serve the practical purpose of splitting the force of the wind allowing smoke to escape unhindered.

35 Gutters are provided at the top and sides of this stack by the moulded stone string projecting diagonally at the bottom – a simple design which prevented rainwater from leaking through the roof.

36 Chimneys produced during the sixteenth century were some of the most attractive ever designed, ranging from the intricate decoration at one end of the century to the near total plainness at the other.

37 An early sixteenth century stack in brick, patterns which were used included diamond, lozenge, circular hole and twisted forms.

38 Another decorative example this time from the Elizabethan age, chimney stacks often had single, double or quadruple stacks in one design.

31

32
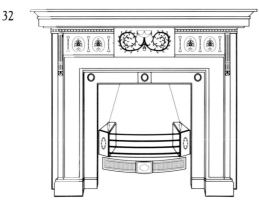

33

CHIMNEYS AND STACKS

34 35
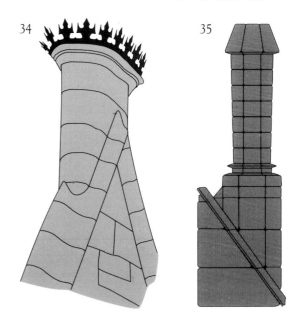

36

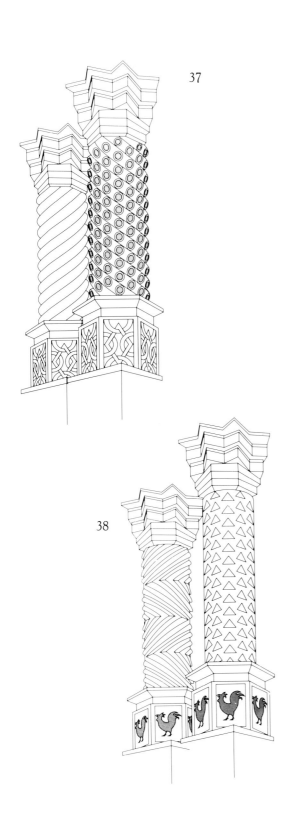

37

38

PARAPETS

39

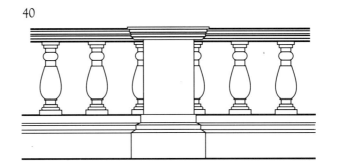

40

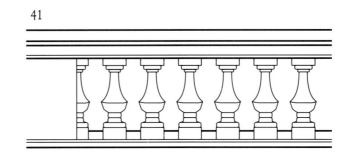

41

39 *From Elizabethan times some kind of parapet or balustrade was built around the top of the outside walls of a house. This Jacobean design shows strapwork typical of the riotous and varied approach during this and the Elizabethan period.*

40 *An Inigo Jones design of the early seventeenth century – the classical parapet had horizontal mouldings top and bottom and a balustrade of vase-shaped balusters.*

41 *A late seventeenth century parapet, blocked at intervals with solid stone forms – these were lined up with the order column below, if one were used, and might be decorated with sculpture.*

GLOSSARY OF ARCHITECTURAL TERMS

This should not be regarded as a full wordstore of architectural expressions. Most words here are listed because of their connection or association with country houses and similar buildings.

ABUTMENT: Masonry (stone or brickwork) placed so as to counteract the lateral thrust of an arch or vault.

ACROTERIA: Plinths, either for statues or ornaments, placed in certain neo-Classical buildings at ends and apex of a pediment.

ADAM, ROBERT: See under 'Great Builders'.

ADDORSED, AFFRONTED: Description of pair of carved figures, usually animals, symmetrically facing each other, or back-to-back.

ANCONES: Brackets or consoles flanking a doorway supporting a cornice. Also, the projections left on stone blocks to allow them to be hoisted into position.

ANTIFIXAE: Ornamental or carved blocks at the edge of a roof to conceal tile-ends.

APEX, APEX STONE: The highest point of a gable. Apex stone also called the saddle-stone.

ARABESQUE: Intricate, often ornate surface decoration using geometrical patterns and flowing lines.281

ARCADE: Range of arches on piers or columns, free-standing or attached to a wall. Also, a covered passage with shops on either or both sides.

ARCH: Self-supporting curved masonry structure over a door or other aperture in a wall. Consists of keystone and voussoirs resting on imposts. Many types of arch exist, including three- and four-centred arches, basket, lancet, horseshoe, ogee, Tudor.

ARCHITRAVE: The lowest of three parts of an entablature. More recently, the moulded frame surrounding a doorway or window.

ASHLAR: Blocks of masonry given even faces and square edges to facilitate building with them, in contrast to unhewn stone.

ASTRAGAL: A decorative circular moulding. Also, the (usually) thin timber glazing bars on sashweight windows.

BAILEY: Courtyard or open space within a stone-built castle.

BALCONY: A platform projecting from a wall with railing or balustrade.

BALUSTRADE: A series of small pillars supporting a rail or coping at the edge of a terrace, balcony or roof.

BARGEBOARDS, VERGEBOARDS: Projecting, often decorated, boards forming an inverted V under a gable to conceal the ends of the horizontal roof timbers.

BAROQUE ARCHITECTURE: Complex, ornate architecture of the seventeenth and eighteenth centuries, more widespread in Europe than in Britain. Sir Christopher Wren, Nicholas Hawksmoor and Sir John Vanbrugh, among others, are Britain's most notable exponents.

BASEMENT: Lowest storey of a building, often partly below ground. But it is a living and working area, distinct from the cellar.

BATTER: Inclined wallface.

BATTLEMENT: Parapet with regular indentations or embrasures. Raised parts are called merlons. Also called crenellation.

BAY: Vertical division of a country house or other building, measured in numbers of windows or other repeated feature. An eight-bay house, for instance, has eight windows on its facade.

BAY, BOW WINDOW: Curved, sometimes angular, projection of a house front with windows. On upper floor only, oriel window.

BEAM: Strong horizontal timber supporting upper floor or roof.

BELLCOTE, BELL GABLE: Roof framework to hang bells from.

BLIND WINDOW: Window elements (surround, astragals, mullions, matt black paint) put on a wall to look like a window, but without an aperture. Used to creat symmetry or special effect.

BOISERIE: French word for elaborately decorated panelling or wainscotting.

BONNET TILE: Rounded tile to join plain tiles along roof hips.

BOX: Small country dwelling, shooting lodge, rectory.

BRACE: Diagonally-placed timber to strengthen a timber frame.

BRESSUMER: Horizontal timber carrying brickwork or masonry above it. A timber lintel.

BUTTRESS: Important feature of Gothic architecture. Mass of masonry placed against thin wall to give strength and counterract lateral roof thrust. Buttress types include angle, clasping, diagonal, flying, lateral, pier and setback.

CAMPANILE: Italian word for bell-tower, usually square, an architectural feature used to enhance certain country houses in Britain in the late eighteenth, early nineteenth centuries.

CAPITAL: The carved or ornate top of a column. Innumerable designs exist, and would provide a chapter of their own.

CASEMENT WINDOW: Most recent window type (preceeded by sashweight), with timber or metal frame, where part of or all the window opens outward or inward on side-hinges like a door.

CASTLE: Fortified habitation.

CHAMFER: Surface created when the 90 degree edge of stone or timber is cut away, usually at an angle of 45 degrees. Called a hollow chamfer if surface is made concave.

CHIMNEY-BAR: Bar above fireplace aperture carrying front of chimney-breast, the stone or brick structure projecting in to the room which funnels up to form the flue.

COLUMN: Upright member, usually of stone and slightly tapering. Consists of base, shaft and capital and, with other columns, carries an entablature. Most columns belong to one of four orders – Doric, Tuscan, Ionic or Corinthian – or are composite.

COPING: A cap or cover for a wall, often sloping to allow water to run off.

CORBEL: A projecting block, usually of masonry, supporting a beam or other horizontal structure. A series, each projecting slightly more, can be used to build a vault, arch or overhang. Hence – corbel arch, corbel course, corbel ring, corbel table.

CORNICE: Top. projecting section of an entablature. On the sloping sides of a pediment, it is called a raking cornice. Also means any projecting or ornamental moulding at the top of a building, arch or wall.

COVE, COVING: Concave moulding usually placed at junction of walls to ceilings.

CROSS WINDOW: Window with single mullion and transom, so-named because they form a cross.

CROW STEPS, CORBIE STEPS: Stepped gable, mainly found in Scotland.

CRUCKS: Pairs of big, curved upright timbers, called blades, used in Tudor times and earlier to form the basic skeleton of a house.

CUPOLA: A dome, usually on a circular base, often glazed, topping a roof or turret.

CURTAIN-WALL: Thin, non-loadbearing wall of early Gothic churches or, alternatively, the massive high blank protective wall of castles.

DENTIL: Small square ornamental blocks used to enhance entablatures or cornices in certain houses.

DORMER WINDOW: Window placed vertically in a sloping roof, often with a small gable above it.

DRAGON BEAM: Cantilevered beam running diagonally out to the corners of Tudor-era houses to support the first-floor overhang.

DRESSINGS: Stones with a finished face used around an angle, doorway or window.

DRUM: Vertical wall under a dome or cupola.

EAVES: Underpart of a sloping roof where it overhangs a wall.

EGG AND DART: Type of moulding, either plaster or carved wood, with a pattern based on alternate eggs and arrow-heads.

ELEVATION: External faces of a building, and drawings thereof.

ELIZABETHAN AND JACOBEAN ARCHITECTURE: Related styles prevalent in the reign of Elizabeth I and James I, though there was a strong revival of the Jacobean style in Victorian times. Very much native styles of Britain, compared to the neo-Classical styles from the Continent.

EMBRASURE: Recess for window or door in thick-walled castle. Also, opening in a castle parapet.

ENGAGED COLUMN: (Also called applied or attached column). Column attched to, or partly sunk into, a wall, pier or other structure.

ENTABLATURE: Big stone beam forming the top part of an order, or line of columns, in Greek and neo-Classical buildings. Consists of architrave, frieze and cornice.

ENTRESOL: Also mezzanine. Floor or storey built between two main floors.

EXTRADOS: The external curved faced of an arch or vault. The underside is the intrados.

EYE-CATCHER: Also called folly. A decorative small building, often a specially-built sham ruin, in a garden or landscape.

FACADE: Architecturally-emphasised front or face of a building.

FACING: Finish applied to building externally, such as stucco or Roman cement.

FANLIGHT: Window, often semi-circular, above a door. Popular in Georgian and post-Georgian buildings.

FENESTRATION: Window arrangement of a building.

FILLET: Uppermost part of a cornice, sometimes called a listel.

FLAMBOYANT: Very ornate (as the word suggests) later French Gothic style, with intricate, wavy stonework tracery.

FLIGHT: Series of stairs unbroken by a landing.

FLUTING: Shallow, concave grooves running vertically in a column, shaft or pilaster.

FLYING BUTTRESS: See BUTTRESS.

FOLIATED: Carved or decorated with a leaf pattern.

FOLLY: See EYE-CATCHER.

FRENCH WINDOW: Usually a pair of door-sized casement windows opening from a room to an outside terrace or balcony.

FRIEZE: Centre division of an entablature, between the architrave and the cornice. Usually intricately decorated.

GABLE: Triangular top part of a wall at the edge of a, usually, steeply-pitched roof, similar to the pediment in classical architecture. Normally straight-sided, there are however many variants – such as crow-stepped, Dutch, Holburn and other 'shaped gables'. Dormer or oculus windows often form part of gables.

GALLERY: An internal balcony or platform overlooking a larger room – such as a 'minstrels' gallery'. Also a long room, usually on an upper floor, used for entertaining ('long gallery') or for displaying pictures (hence the term 'art gallery').

GARDEROBE: French for wardrobe. Also, medieval name for lavatory.

GARGOYLE: In Gothic buildings, a water spout jutting from a gutter or parapet shaped like a grotesque animal or human.

GLASS: Known and used since Roman times, the use of glass really started to develop from the early nineteenth century onwards, leading to all-glass structures such as Paxton's Crystal Palace (1851).

GOTHIC ARCHITECTURE: Originally from thirteenth century France and called *l'architecture ogivale*, the style was derisively called 'gothic' by post-Renaissance neo-classical Italian architects. But the name, and the style, has vigorously endured in Britain.

GOTHIC REVIVAL, OR GOTHICK: A revival of Gothic architecture in Britain, particularly of features such as lancet windows and crenellated fortifications, from the late eighteenth century onwards.

GROTTO: Artificial cavern, often not even underground, with fountains and pools, etc. Popular in the eighteenth century.

HARLING: Scots term for roughcast.

HARMONIC PROPORTIONS: Architectural concept that room dimensions should be in mathematical relationship to each other to create a harmonic sense of space. Theory greatly developed by Palladio.

HERRINGBONE WORK: Bricks laid in neat zig-zag patterns instead of parallel courses. Often used to infill between timbers in Tudor houses or underfoot in outside courtyards.

HIP: External angle formed by the meeting of two sloping roofs.

HOOD-MOULD: Moulding above a door or window aperture to throw off the rain. Occasionally called label or dripstone.

HYPOCAUST: Underfloor heating-duct system built into many Roman houses. Probably the earliest form of central heating.

IMPOST: The section of a wall, usually with an ornate cornice or moulding, on which the span of an arch appears to rest.

INGLENOOK, INGLENEUK: Recess for bench inside a large fireplace.

INTRADOS: Underside or inner curve of an arch. Also called soffit.

JACOBEAN ARCHITECTURE: See ELIZABETHAN ARCHITECTURE.

JAMB: Vertical face of doorway, archway or window.

JETTY: System on timber-frame buildings whereby beams and joists overhang the external walls of the lower floor so the upper floor is built with a greater floor area. Popular with Elizabethan and Tudor buildings. See DRAGON BEAM.

JOISTS: Parallel horizontal timbers laid between beams or walls of a building to carry the floorboards. Undersides may be left exposed or covered with lath and plaster.

KEYSTONE: Wedge-shaped central stone of an arch or vault. Often ornately carved.

LANCET WINDOW, LANCET ARCH: Windowarch rising to an upper point. Hallmark of much early Gothic architecture.

LATROBE, BENJAMIN HENRY: See 'Great Builders'.

LATTICE WINDOW: Window with leaded lights, usually diamond-shaped, like an open lattice screen.

LE NOTRE, ANDRE: Great French landscape gardener.

LIGHTS: Openings between the mullions and transoms of a window.

LINTEL: Beam of either wood, stone or (today) pre-stressed concrete bridging a door or window opening.

LUCARNE: Small aperture in attic, spire or turret roof. Also French word for dormer window.

MANNERISM: Ornate, overemphasised style derived from the neo-Classical. Predominant in Italy throughout the late sixteenth century. Had some influence on British architects at the time.

MANOR HOUSE: Unfortified, medium-sized house of the later Middle Ages. Predecessor of the great country houses.

MANSARD ROOF: Roof with two angles of slope, steep near the edge, less so at the centre, which allows living room to be built in an attic space. Named after the French architect who invented it.

MANTELPIECE: The frame, of wood, stone or marble, which surrounds a fireplace.

MEZZANINE: See ENTRESOL.

MORTICE AND TENON JOINT: Nail- and glue-free early system to join big house timbers, with a projecting piece (tenon) fitting deeply into a socket (mortice).

MOTTE: Steep mound on which early castles were built, often surrounded by a BAILEY or deep ditch or moat. Hence, motte-and-bailey castle.

MOULDINGS: General term given to decorative or camouflaging projecting members with no inherent structural purposes.

MULLION: Vertical post in timber or stone in Tudor, Elizabethan houses which split the window aperture into smaller lights.

NEO-GOTHIC: See GOTHIC REVIVAL.

NICHE: Vertical recess in a wall or other structure, usually concave and arched and containing a figure, vase or other object.

OCTAGON: Eight-sided building with all sides equal.

OCTASTYLE: A portico with eight frontal columns.

OCULUS: Circular opening or window, particularly in the tympanum of a pediment or in an ornate Holburn or Dutch gable.

OEIL-DE-BOEUF WINDOW: Small, usually oval decorative window.

OEILLET: Small slit or opening in castle fortifications through which arrows or other missiles could be fired.

ORDER: In Greek, Classical and all related architecture, the complete column – consisting of base, shaft, capital and entablature – in one of the five or six accepted modes: Greek Doric, Roman Doric, Corinthian, Ionic, Tuscan and Composite.

ORIEL: See BAY WINDOW.

PANTILE: Roofing tile with s-shaped section.

PARAPET: Low wall, sometimes crenellated, placed at the edge of a roof or other location where there is a steep drop.

PARGETTING: External plastering, often decorative, of an early timber-frame house. The tradesmen were pargetters, and the name comes from the French 'par jeter' – by throwing.

PARQUET: Floor of thin hardwood, highly polished, often laid in complex patterns.

PAVILION: Lightly constructed, often ornamental building used as a summer house.

PEDESTAL: Strong base supporting a column of statue.

PEDIMENT: In classical and neo-classical architecture, the low-pitched gable over a portico, usually above an entablature supported by columns. Also a similar but smaller feature above a single door or window. In the Baroque era, pediments became very ornate and complex, sometimes without apex or base, the former called an open-topped pediment, the latter an open-bed pediment.

PEEL-TOWER: A small tower house suitable for defence, generally found in Northern England and Scotland.

PICTURESQUE: A unenduring late-eighteenth century style of English architecture which brought together often clashing styles in one building to achieve an intriguing visual effect.

PIER: Solid, blocky masonry support, quite unlike a column.

PILASTER: Shallow pseudo-column or pier projecting from a wall and, correctly, belonging to one of the orders. Widely used on neo-Classical and Georgian houses to create the visual effect of a portico without having to build one.

PILLAR: Upright, free-standing structure which, not being a column, needs neither to be cylindrical or to conform to any of the orders.

PLINTH: Projecting base of a wall or pedestal.

PLINTH BLOCK: Item at the base of door architrave, mantelpiece against which skirting board is stopped.

POINTING: The exposed mortar finishing between bricks or blocks. Various types of pointing exist, including flush pointing, recessed, hungry-joint, ribbon pointing, etc.

PORTICO, PORCH, PORTE-COCHERE: Various types of entrances to buildings. Portico is impressive, with columns, pediment and other refinements. Porte-cochere allows a vehicle to stop underneath it. A porch is much simpler than either.

QUADRANGLE: Rectangular courtyard enclosed on all sides by buildings, or an open space in the centre of a single building.

QUOINS: Visually-effective dressed stones at the corners of buildings, often laid in alternate sizes to enhance the effect.

RAINWATER HEAD: Box-shaped metal structure, often ornately decorated, through which gutter-collected rainwater off the roof is channelled into the downpipe.

RAYONNANT: Early French Gothic architectural style, which used many radiating lines, hence the name.

RENDERING: Plastering (generally) of an exterior wall.

RETAINING WALL: Wall, usually inclined, built to retain water or an earthen embankment.

ROCOCO ARCHITECTURE: The final phase of Baroque architecture, which emphasised lightness and pastel colours. Had very little impact in Britain.

ROOF: There are more types and variations of roof construction than there is space in this book to deal with. Most roofs of country houses are, however, of timber construction with slate, tile or other mineral covering. Types include king-post roof, arched brace roof, hammerbeam roof or crown post roof. Rarely if ever have flat-roofed country houses been built.

ROTUNDA: Circular building, usually domed and with a colonnade.

RUSTICATION: Masonry cut in big blocks, separated by deep chamfered joints, to give a rich texture to an outside wall. The outer faces of the blocks can be finished in various ways, including smooth, vermiculated, cyclopean, diamond-pointed or many more.

SASH WINDOWS: Imported from Holland, sash windows are timber frames which slide up and down in grooves, counterbalanced by unseen sash weights.

SERLIANA: An archway or window with three openings, the middle one higher and wider than the two which flank it. The three openings are framed or separated by columns, the outer two topped by entablatures and cornices. Also known as a Venetian window, it was originally conceived by Sebastiano Serlio, was much used by Palladio and became a hallmark of seventeenth and eighteenth century Palladianism in Britain.

SOFFIT: The underside of an arch or vault or, more generally, the underside of any architectural element.

SOLOMONIC COLUMN: A column twisted like barley-sugar, supposed to have been used in Solomon's temple.

SPIRE: Tall, pyramidal or conical structure rising from a tower or turret, usually of a church and ending in a sharp point. A small spire rising, say, above a roof pier is called a spirelet.

STAIR, STAIRCASE: Staircases have existed for 6000 years and, although earlier ones mainly of masonry, today they are of timber or of precast concrete. Ornate, complex staircases were often the most important internal feature of a country house.

STOP-CHAMFER, OR BROACH-STOP: Ingenious shaping of brick or stone to return a chamfered edge (of, say, a hexagonal chimney-stack) to dead square.

STRAPWORK: Decorative bands, first made in France or Holland, used in Elizabethan times to decorate walls above head height. Usually intricately carved in wood or plaster.

STRING COURSE: A horizontal continuous band, either of contrasting stone or brick, projecting slightly from a wall. Sometimes moulded, it gives the impression of a shallow ledge and helps reduce the blank uniformity of a facade.

STUCCO: Originally Italian word meaning very smooth plasterwork.

TEMPLATE: Also called pad stone. Stone block installed at top of rubble or brick wall to carry weight of joists or roof trusses.

TERRACE: Level promenade at the front or rear of a country house. Gardens set on several different levels are often called terraced gardens.

THATCH: Straw or reed roof covering, used on early manor houses.

TIMBER-FRAMING: Historically, this refers to timber Tudor-era houses, with strong oak vertical and horizontal timbers infilled with 'wattle and daub' (plaster with coloured finish) or later with bricks and other materials.

TOWER HOUSE: Medieval Scots fortified house with walls often seven feet thick and the living quarters on the first floor and above.

TRACERY: Ornamental intersecting decoration, much used in early Gothic church windows.

TRANSOM: Horizontal wood or stone bar to divide a window aperture into separate light. See MULLION.

TURRET: Small, slender tower.

TYMPANUM: Triangular or segmental space enclosed by the mouldings of a pediment. Also, area between a doorway lintel and the arch above it.

VAULT: Arched ceiling or roof, of stone, brickwork or other materials, often associated with cellars or other underground structures.

VENETIAN DOOR, VENETIAN WINDOW: See SERLIANA.

VILLA: A country house, though the size and grandeur of a house termed a villa has varied much over the centuries.

VOUSSOIR: Brick or wedge-shaped stone forming one of the units of an arch.

WAINSCOT: Timber lining to walls.

WATTLE AND DAUB: Early method of infilling wall gaps in Early English and Tudor timber-frame houses.

WINDOWS: Three main types have been used in country houses: early lights, with mullions and transoms; sashweight windows and casement windows.